£8.95

CW00920046

THE RAILWAYS OF HULL

By

C. T. Goode

Cover picture: *A workers' train bound for the Brough aircraft factory crosses Anlaby Road behind an ex GC A5 tank engine.*

ISBN 1 870313 11 9
72 Woodland Drive, Anlaby, Hull. HU10 7HX

Produced by
Burstwick Publicity Services,
Burstwick, Hull

Contents

Foreword

My first experience of the railways of Hull came after 1955, when I was appointed to teach at Riley High School. There the lads, who came in each day from far and wide had a glorious excuse for lateness, as 'the bridge was up' or, more commonly, 'the gates were closed'. Those from eastern parts had a choice of various bridges over the river and crossings to blame. I spent a lot of time at the school, then at the corner of Boulevard, teaching in a front classroom overlooking Anlaby Road crossing, and it was quite possible to keep a log of daytime train movements aided by a couple of keen enthusiasts by the window.

After 1960 I moved to the gentler climes of Bridlington High School, to which resort I travelled daily in term time by rail, using the new dmus for nine years and supervising the eighty or so girls who were collected from wayside stations. Not a bad life for a railway buff!

New subjects to write about are becoming thin on the ground, and most places have been covered. This book may thus be the last of a little series of works which I have enjoyed writing and which I trust readers have enjoyed as well. If any one can suggest subjects as yet uncovered, I shall be pleased to hear from them, as well as comments, constructive or otherwise, on this effort.

C. Tony Goode.

Anlaby 1992.

The Railways of Hull

Hull is at first sight well and truly out on a geographical limb to an outsider who might well wonder why such a place came to exist away from the usual runs of commercial contact. Arrival from the west has always been a long-drawn out and tedious progress from Doncaster by rail, a point where civilisation seems to keep a last bastion and from where the long railway ride to Hull is a monotonous last straw with the train passing mile after mile of river alongside. The motorway offers better views and more variety, with not much traffic or clutter. Its only major drawback seems to be that of petering out into an A road some twelve miles outside the city, as if to admonish the traveller for venturing so far.

The Humber Bridge, of course, brings traffic in from the south directly over the river, though one feels that, even after ten or more years of existance, things are not quite right geographically; the direction is wrong and, in any case, the volume of traffic is not worthy of consideration.

Hull's secret is its waterways and, ultimately, the sea down the Humber estuary. The place first claimed attention as a landing point at the mouth of the little river Hull on the north bank of the Humber, for the monks of Meaux had come here from France to settle, which they did to the north, building Meaux abbey. By 1269 the Hull had become navigable for traffic to and from Beverley, while in 1293 the village of Hull became the property of King Edward I who obtained it from the aforementioned monks. Thus, at this early date Hull became 'royal' and was the part of Yorkshire which received goods by water from York through Selby which were collected for larger vessels at Hull. The ball was now set rolling, with a royal charter permitting two markets per week. One of the major imports of the period was wine, against the export of wool, lead and leather.

King Edward I had moved north by road in April 1300, taking his route through Lincolnshire and crossing the Humber on 26th. May by the ferry between Barton and Hessle, whence he would have taken the high road to Beverley. However, he diverted to inspect his newly formed borough of Kingston-upon-Hull, more than likely the first Royal visitor to the place, and one which soon shared its benefits in the various improvements which took place in such matters as street paving. Access to the town by road was extremely difficult and of course the commercial traffic was water-borne. Representations were made to Parliament over the difficulties, and in 1302 the Rector of North Cave and one Gotfrid de Hotham were commissioned to plan roads towards Hull. The upshot was the creation of three major routes from the river Hull leading out along Whitefriargate and Carr lane to Anlaby and the Via Regia from Hessle to Beverley; the second to Beverley through Chariot street and Prospect street and a third crossing the river at North bridge and out into Holderness at Bilton. Crossing the estuary was done by means of the Royal Ferry, mentioned above, though this became rather expensive, no

Rebuilt ex H&B 0.6.0 No. 2473 on an Up goods train at Cottingham South.
T. Rounthwaite

doubt because of the royal patronage; another ferry was founded by King Edward II between Hull and Barton at a rate of ½ d per head or one penny if with a horse. This was known as the South Ferry, while that across the river Hull's mouth was the North.

At this time, around 1377, the population of Hull was roughly 2,000 and matters proceeded steadily until about 1790, with good, humble folk moving from place to place on foot, often covering great distances, and the not so humble and often not so good using horse power. After 1780 the Turnpike Act came into force leading to the improvement of roads, often by the application of tolls levied for London and the south went over the water to Barton and on by coach, while a daily coach ran to Selby to connect with vehicles for Liverpool and Manchester. A vehicle also ran to Doncaster, crossing the Booth Ferry.

In 1833 the 'Express' was plying between Hull and Scarborough, with connections as far as Edinburgh, leaving the Victoria Hotel at 6 a.m. and reaching Scarborough at 12.15 p.m., going forward at 4 p.m. The return trip left Scarborough at 6 a.m., arriving in Hull at noon with an advertised connection via Barton arriving in London at noon on the next day. The 'British Queen' left Bridlington at 7 a.m., travelling by way of Brandesburton to reach Hull at 11a.m., returning at 4 p.m. for a four hour run back to the 'Stirling Castle' Hotel in Bridlington. This was one of the two companies which provided the service.

In the same year the 'Pelham', a light four inside coach left Boston at 6 a.m., running to New Holland and reaching Hull at 3.30 p.m. to connect with the coaches for Bridlington and York. These would be the 'Magna Charter' and 'Trafalgar' which left from the 'Cross Keys' in Hull. There were three departures for York, at 6 a.m., 11.35 a.m. and 4 p.m., of which two were mail coaches. In 1835 the 'Rapid' left the 'Cross Keys' for Manchester, certainly a rather daunting trip which sallied forth at 6.45 a.m., calling at Cave, Howden and Booth Ferry, where half an hour was allowed for breakfast, then on to Snaith, Pontefract, Wakefield, Dewsbury, Mirfield, Huddersfield, Marsden, Upper Mills and Ashton, reaching Manchester at 7 p.m., the vehicle setting out at 5.45 a.m. on the next day. One trusts that the seats were well upholstered. Much of this early 'National Bus' form of network was operated by Messrs. Geldard & Chaffer of Hull, and to enable the lucky folk of that town to gain the Midlands and South West of the country, it was possible to catch a coach from Barton at 8 a.m. for Leicester, arriving at 8.30 p.m. through Grantham and Melton Mowbray. From Leicester a whole range of journeys led to places such as Coventry, Oxford, Bath, Birmingham, Worcester and Wales.

Hull was now linked with the rest of civilisation, albeit slow but sure.

Ex GC Class 04 No. 6583 on a Down coal train at Weedley. *T. Rounthwaite*

Steam packet boats were to be seen at Hull from about 1815, with services to London, Selby and York. In that year the 'Caledonian' began to ply between Hull and Selby. A packet boat, the 'Eclipse' based in Huddersfield, transferred passengers to or from the Manchester coach which called at the canalside at Snaith, to Goole, Ferrybridge and Leeds, Thorne, Doncaster and Sheffield, though presumably not on the same run.

At this distance there is something quaint and distinctly charming about all the pottering about in stage coaches and fussy little steam boats; the reality was discomfort, delay and acute cold in the worst months of the year. For ten years to 1837 there was wrangling over whether it was better to send the mails to London via New Holland rather than Barton, to gain or lose three miles. In the end it was said that the railway, when it came, would reduce the journey time from eighteen hours to eight, even by a circuitous route. The writing was on the wall for the old mail coaches and the railway era was dawning.

First railways to Hull

Today's Hull is over ten times that of the population in 1800, when, as already mentioned, affairs were essentially parochial, with only local traffic and the place largely unvisited from the outside; however, the railway was soon to put an end to this state of affairs. First in line was the Stockton & Darlington in 1825, to be followed by the Liverpool & Manchester, the Leeds & Manchester and, to bring the modern wonder even nearer, the Leeds & Selby, promoted by Benjamin Gott and surveyed by George Stephenson in 1825. His plan included three inclines out of Leeds, worked by stationary engines, two west facing, a method which, even in the infancy of railways, was somewhat frowned upon. Originally a Leeds & Hull Railway Company had been formed in 1824, but with the presence of a free means of transport, namely the Ouse from Selby, the idea of going all the way by rail was shelved. In 1829 a second survey was obtained from James Walker who removed the inclined planes in exchange for bridges crossing the Great North, Wetherby and Selby roads. There was also a tunnel at the Leeds end and a suitable wharf by the Ouse at Selby. An Act for all this was obtained in 1830 and the line was opened to passengers on 22nd. September 1834, with the freight following on 16th. December. For a time the line was closed while the stone sleepers, which gave a harsh ride, were replaced by wooden ones.

The Hull end of things was not at all happy with the state of affairs which left passengers at Selby with the prospect of a journey of anything up to five hours spent in surveying the sand banks, mud flats and reeds on the packet journey, so that there was vigorous vocal promotion for the

A rare view of the experimental Kitson-Still locomotive on a goods trom York, near Cottingham. *Coll: C. T. Goode*

completion of the line, if not financial. To the fore were two bankers, Messrs. G. Liddell and J. Hewood. These gentlemen, along with John Smith of Melton Garth attended a promotional meeting in Selby and similar meetings in Hull, at one of which twenty volunteers were demanded who might subscribe £1,000 each to the cause. They were eventually found and Henry Broadley, the landowner, put up £2,000 in a fine gesture. These was, however, much opposition from landowners, a common drawback to such prospects at this time, the Raikes family of Welton objecting to the passage of the line through their estate. They were bought off for £10,000 and a promise not to build a station at Welton, which would in any case have been a long way distant. Brough was chosen as the place of honour instead. An Act was obtained for the line on 21st. June 1836, with a working capital of £533,333. Mr. Walker, the Engineer, opted for a straight and almost level run of 18 miles instead of deviating somewhat to serve the Caves, a move taken to offset any possile competition from other interests later on. The total length of line was 31 miles, with three water crossings. The two bridges over the Derwent and canal at Broomfleet were identical in form. The original survey suggested that the line ran north of Hessle road at the Hull end, south of Coltman street and terminating near to Mytongate bridge, almost anticipating the later run to Paragon station. However, a riverside route was chosen to end up at English street near the Humber Dock. It is interesting that, although there were no obvious physical difficulties, the line took four years to construct.

The Opening Ceremony

Wednesday, 1st. July 1840 was the day fixed for the Grand Opening of the new line, when four engines, the 'Kingston', 'Exley', 'Andrew Marvell', 'Prince' and 'Selby' were employed, along with four trains of 32 coaches. A public holiday was declared and almost all businesses were closed, During the morning there had been heavy rain which fortunately eased off during the afternoon when the first train left at 12.15 p.m. for Selby, taking almost two hours on the journey. However, the return journey with 'Prince' was made in one hour and five minutes, a vast improvement. On return a banquet was to be found for the guests on the upper floor of the goods warehouse where a cold meal for 760 was set out, in charge of the Bishop, the collation covering 15 tables. After grace by the Rev. Bromby of Holy Trinity, many of the guests at the gathering, chaired by Henry Broadley MP added their speeches to the event. The vicar contributed his comments and hoped that the railway, if it had to run on Sundays, would contrive to allow its servants to attend church at some time during the day. Alderman George Hudson, that great man, responded to the toast and briefly mentioned his other railway concerns in Yorks. and Lancs., stating that, in reality, the talents of Mr. George Stephenson deserved the highest compliments; noble praise for a partner.

The 'Hull Herald' gave an exhaustive description of the original terminus. The chief building of white stone was 100ft. by 70 ft. housing the offices, both for parcels and passengers, two waiting rooms and a passageway of 50 ft. by 12 ft. Above were rooms for the directors and secretaries, more waiting rooms and an office. Of the operational side of the station, the article reads as follows:

'The passage already noticed leads also to the passengers' shed, a very spacious, lofty, light and, for its purpose, handsome structure. It is 170 ft. long by 72 ft. wide, and of the extreme height of about 40 ft. The roof is supported by 22 iron columns. This building is lighted by 22 windows, and the west end is perfectly open. On each side are raised platforms 12 ft. wide and extending the entire length of the building for the convenience of stepping into and out of the passengers' carriages. Between these platforms are four lines of railway, with convenience for removing carriages from one line to an other. On the north side of the shed are several large doors, opening to a flagged footpath six feet in breadth and a carriageway treble that width.'

 Stations between Hull and Selby on opening were at Hessle, Ferriby and

Brough as nowadays, then Staddlethorpe (Gilberdyke). as Broomfleet was yet to come in 1861, Eastrington, Howden & Bubwith and Cliffe, which became Hemingbrough in later days. Wressle was also to appear in due course.

The first trains were halted outside the station in Hull and drawn in by cable and stationary engine, though later on the engine was detached and run to the rear for it to push the train up to the buffer stops. This was either a matter of safety or, more likely, to avoid blocking in the arriving engine longer than necessary. Apparently hats were lost in great numbers by the gentlemen travelling on the trains, and on Sundays many people took the train ride to sample the delights of this mode of travelling, with a first class single to Leeds costing eight shillings, while the second and third fares were 6s.6d. and 4s.6d. respectively. Excursion rates were numerous; those who went to market in Hull on Tuesdays and travelled on the 9 a.m. could return free on the 3 p.m., an offer which was known to attract up to 400 passengers from Leeds to Hull and back.

On 7th. September 1840 a train ran through the back wall of Hull station and into the passage beyond it. After this debacle, trains were brought to a stand before they uncoupled and always brought in by a cable.

There came into being a short period of agreement with the Manchester

Class X2 2-2-2T pressed into passenger service near Cottingham *C.T. Goode*

& Leeds Company over joint working, and in 1843 the directors suggested amalgamation, a move which the shareholders rejected, so that the idea fell through. However, in the following year the suggestion was raised again, this time pointing towards a union with the York & North Midland, a move which came from George Hudson who, having already bought over the Leeds & Selby, needed the Hull & Selby for his collection to fend off any building contenders in his spheres of interest. And so, from 1st July 1845 the Hull & Selby was handed over to Hudson's York & North Midland, just five years after its opening, much to the disapproval of the Manchester & Leeds, later Lancashire & Yorkshire, who felt that they had the greater right to the acquisition, even though territorially the successful contender was more favourably disposed towards the folk of Hull.

The L & Y would not, in the eyes of many, have been a worthy successor to the H & S, as that company was actively promoting Goole up river as a port, to Hull's detriment.

The Bridlington (Burlington) branch ran due north from a junction at Dairycoates, known locally as the 'straight line' through Cottingham and Beverley. It was given an Act on 30th. June 1845, the day before the Y & NM had obtained its Act for a line from Seamer, near Scarborough, to Bridlington, most fortuitously to give through running between the two resorts. There were 37 crossings of roadways on the proposed branch, and on the opening day, 2nd. November 1846, with George Hudson present, the first train rolled northwards, comprising a mighty load of three engines hauling 66 carriages. Eighteen months later the portion of line south of Cottingham closed to passenger traffic, due to the opening of the new line into the town proper to serve the new terminus at Paragon street. The original 'straight line' was left for excursions and goods traffic which would surprise road users who had forgotten the existence of the crossings; but more of that presently.

Removal of trains from the old terminus became necessary when their number became too many and when it was found that traffic from Beverley and Bridlington did not materialise, as the dockland station was too inconvenient for them, especially those who lived in the plushier, west part of the town. The Old station was enlarged and improved as a goods station, with further land adjacent bought for its use.

The new Paragon Street Station

In 1847 the Y & NM secured an Act for the construction of the new Paragon street station and Hotel on 2½ acres, and on 13th. and 14th. October 1854, Queen Victoria, Prince Albert and five Royal children stayed at the new premises, thereafter to be known as the Royal Station Hotel, on what was possibly the first ever royal mini-break.

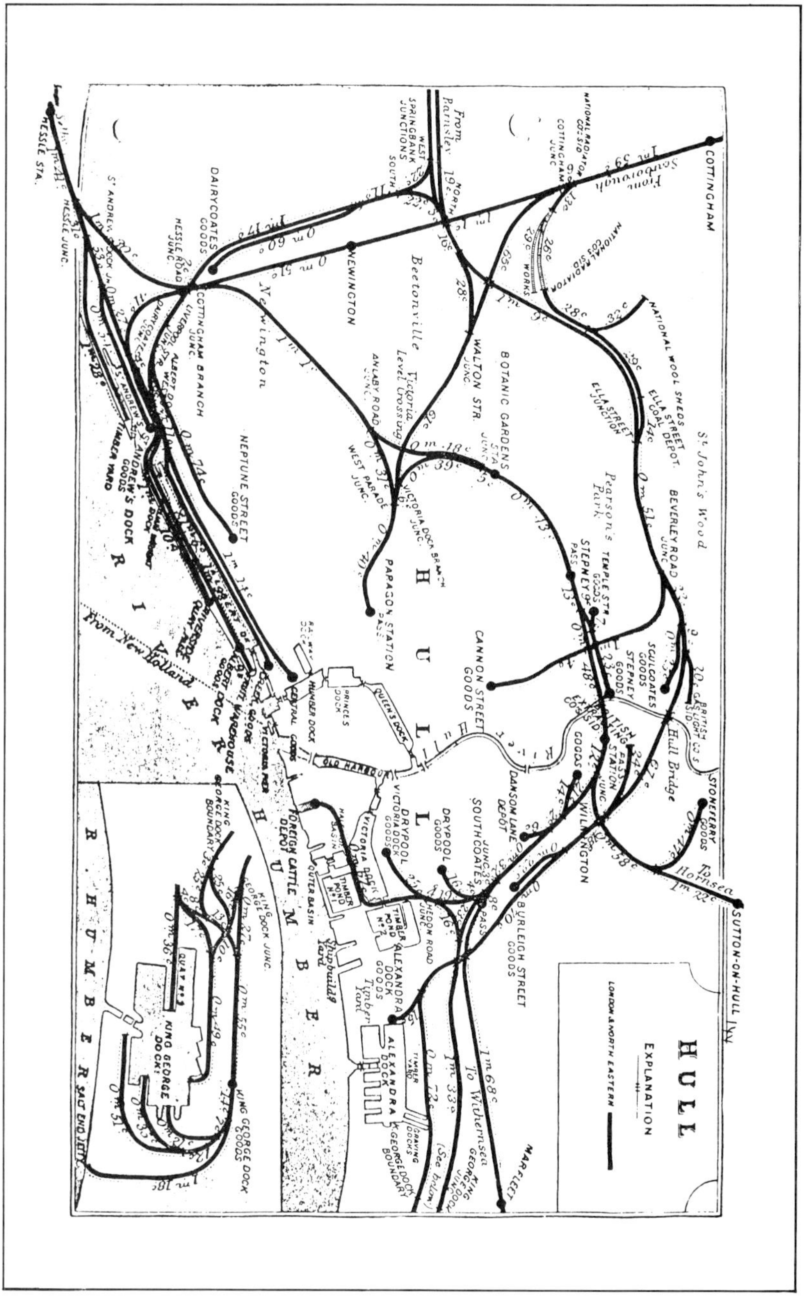
HULL
EXPLANATION
LONDON & NORTH EASTERN
COTTINGHAM
SUTTON-ON-HULL
STONEFERRY GOODS
MARFLEET
To Withernsea
To Hornsea
From Scarborough
From Barnsley
NEWINGTON
DAIRYCOATES GOODS
HESSLE STA.
HESSLE JUNC.
HESSLE ROAD JUNC.
COTTINGHAM BRANCH JUNC.
NEPTUNE STREET GOODS
ST ANDREW'S DOCK
BOTANIC GARDENS STA.
WALTON STR. JUNC.
ANLABY ROAD JUNC.
WEST PARADE JUNC.
PARAGON STATION
CANNON STREET GOODS
BEVERLEY ROAD JUNC.
STEPNEY
SCULCOATES GOODS
WILMINGTON
DANSOM LANE DEPOT
DRYPOOL GOODS
SOUTHCOATES
BURLEIGH STREET GOODS
ALEXANDRA DOCK
VICTORIA DOCK
HUMBER DOCK
PRINCES DOCK
QUEEN'S DOCK
OLD HARBOUR
FOREIGN CATTLE DEPOT
KING GEORGE DOCK
KING GEORGE DOCK GOODS
KING GEORGE DOCK JUNC.
Hull Bridge
Pearson's Park
St John's Wood
Newington
Beetonville
H U L L
H U M B E R
R I V E R
From New Holland

The opening of the new station occurred without undue ceremony, with around 500 assembled to see the first train leave at 6.20 a.m., delayed for some time as the engine was derailed on its way to couple up to the carriages. There was also delay in opening the premises which had been scheduled for readiness the previous August; however, a dispute with the masons employed slowed things down and the new hotel was not in fact ready on the first day. This had 80 bedrooms, and the main feature was a quadrangle inside of 60 ft. square, paved in marble beneath a skylight glazed with ground glass. The stone used in both buildings was the same as that used for the Houses of Parliament, and came from Anston, near Worksop, Notts. Initially there were five lines between the platforms and a shed on the north side by West street, half of which was used by engines, the other for sheltering carriages and omnibuses-the infant coach station of today. The original station building and hotel were designed by G.T. Andrews of York and forms a five part composite of a centre portion of two storeys with porte cochère which is now glazed in as an office, two single storey wings and two two storey terminal buildings, one of which forms part of the hotel and which was later raised up by one floor. The centre block is five windows wide, while the connecting wings have ten windows and a centre doorway. The end buildings have three and five windows respectively. The whole of the original buildings ran east-west parallel with the lines of their southern side. The bulk of these buildings remains and is now, among other things, a parcels office. The hotel is being rebuilt and has just been ' topped out' after a sad and destructive fire in October 1990. It is hoped to open once more in late 1992 with the original facade retained. The original facade to Paragon square was three storeys plus added attics and a recessed centre of five bays between two projecting wings, each of two windows in width. Two wings and an attic storey were added about 1936.

The original entrance to the station and offices stretched westwards beyond the hotel and was eventually hidden behind cinema, showrooms and a college. The newer entrance from Paragon square with booking office were added between 1903 and 1908. The booking hall is tiled throughout and, to date, is preserved as it was originally. The iron canopy and clock over the entry on the Paragon square side was removed in 1962 to be replaced by the shoe box office construction of the period, mounted on stilts to afford some protection to visiting road vehicles beneath it.

Queen Victoria visited Hull to tour the town and docks, an event of which only the Mayor was apparently notified just ten days beforehand, causing much fluttering and preparation, purchasing of materials and piles of timber which appeared in the station yard and in the streets ready to make the arches and awnings. Many flocked to the town to witness the first royal visit for two centuries and, as it was the Fair week, takings here were substantial. It was no doubt hoped that Her Majesty would visit the ground and take a spin on the mechanical horses!

The royal train left Selby at 4.59 p.m., was through Howden at 5.08 p.m. and reached Hull at 5.45 p.m. where the Queen and Party with Albert and the Princesses on her left and the Prince of Wales and Prince Albert on her right received local worthies and heard their speeches of welcome before they had changed from their travelling clothes. The party had alighted on the north side and were greeted by Miss Ivatts and Mr. Jordan, the lessees of the hotel, who had made a suite ready. A Throne room had been set up in the south east corner of the hotel where the Queen would be able to receive further local dignitaries.

The Hull & Holderness Railway was independently conceived, and a prospectus was issued in 1852 produced by its founder, Alderman Bannister and with a directing board of local worthies, including Sir Thomas Constable, the Mayor and Sherriff of Hull, John Hildyard of Winestead, Samuel Priestman of Sutton, J. W. Pease of Hesslewood and C. R. Ringrose of Tranby, all gentlemen with suitable money and vision to secure a good launch for the company. An Act was obtained on 8th. July 1853 for a line running from Great Union street, through Hedon and Preston and villages to Patrington, terminating by the sea at Withernsea where, in 1851, the population numbered 109. Arrangements were already in hand for connection to the East Dock branch of the Y & NM, with an option on running thereover into Paragon street station. In the event, passenger trains began running independently from 28th. June 1854, using the company's own engines and carriages along a single line which, due to the easy terrain, cost a mere £5,000 per mile to build. Traffic was brisk, especially in the season, and in January 1860 the NER took over the running of things, using Paragon station as from 1862, round about which time official amalgamation took place.

On the opening day of the Hull & Holderness, the inaugural train departed from Paragon at 11.20 a.m., first calling at Victoria Dock station. During the celebrations, part of the marquee put up for the luncheon party collapsed. Initially there were 5 or 6 trains each way, including two which were non-stop. On market day returns were issued at 1⅓ times the single rate. There were two early stations whch soon disappeared in the line's history, at Winestead and Hollym Gate, the latter just short of Withernsea and which had trains on Tuesdays and Fridays only. Cuthbert Broderick, the designer of Hull Town Hall, built the station at Withernsea, also the Station hotel opposite, later the Queen's. In 1902 the hotel, with three acres of land, was bought by Mr. James Reckitt and given to the Hull Royal Infirmary for use as a convalescent home.

Hedon station pre 1914, with old NE No. 156 approaching on a Hull train.
Coll: A. Sanderson

The Hull & Holderness Railway

Hull & Holderness trains started from a rather nebulous site on a corner of Victoria Dock, turning east near the point where the later Southcoates station was situated. The Y & NM ran its East Dock branch round from Paragon street station, first westwards, then north, east and south through the stations of Stepney and Sculcoates to reach Southcoates and Victoria Dock, where a stretch of line was jointly owned. Trains could stop at level crossings on request, as at Anlaby road, Cemetery Gates and Hessle road. This line opened on 1st. June 1853 for passengers and a month earlier for goods; H & H trains used it first, but surprisingly not availing themselves of Paragon, as neither did the Y & NM services which, instead, chose the old station belonging to the old H & S by the Humber Dock which was reopened, trains crossing the line to Bridlington on the level at Victoria Crossing. The service on the East Dock branch was at two hourly intervals, beginning at 6 a.m. out from Manor House and 7 a.m. from Victoria Dock. It proved unsuccessful, was reduced from seven to four trains and discontinued in 1854, leaving the East Dock branch untraversed by passenger traffic for ten years. The policy at this time was rather strange, to say the least. The Y & NM leased Victoria Dock station to the H & H for a yearly payment of £4,000, and that company was the sole occupant from 1st November 1854, giving Hull two terminal stations, in use at the same time for ten years or so. By 1864 the Victoria Dock branch had been doubled and a connecting curve near to the dock enabled Withernsea trains to run to and from Paragon station for the next hundred years or so. The curve was set to open on 1st. July 1863, but the official inspection found the signalling hardly up to scratch and use was delayed until 1st. June 1864. The old H & H engine shed at Victoria Dock, erected in 1858 was removed to Lockington station when redundant and was used as a garden shed.

Crowds and crowds 'Reckitts' outing to Scarborough at Southcoates in 1912.
Coll: A. Sanderson

Withernsea station was set some way back from the pier, so that, in the early days a bell was rung 15 minutes before departures to alert the tardy, who were either quaffing ale or relaxing to the Quadrille Band in the Garden Salon nearby.

The Hull & Hornsea Railway

There were two forays into Holderness by independent companies. The second of these, the Hull & Hornsea, received its Act on 30th. June 1862 and was authorised to raise a total capital of £93,000. The line was opened for passenger traffic on 28th. March 1864, the first casualty, if such might be called, being the inspecting officer, Col. Rich who fell into the Sutton Drain while checking a bridge. Initially trains terminated at Wilmington, just short of the junction with the East Dock branch, until they could run to Paragon station over the newly doubled line from 1st. July 1864, with a full service, plus the Withernsea trains diverted from the outpost of Victoria Dock which cannot have been convenient for many folk. The station here was thereafter closed. The original Wilmington station was round the corner on the branch beyond the junction. The line cost much more to build than anticipated, so that the company was floundering from the outset. Approaches were made to the NER who were working the trains in any case. The name behind the idea of a Hornsea line was that of Mr. Joseph Wade, a Hornsea resident and Hull timber merchant, who was able to convince various influential people that Hornsea had more to offer than Withernsea, not a difficult task, one might suspect. Unfortunately it seemed from the outset that the townsfolk had little interest in periodic influxes of tourists, and there was reluctance to take the line down from Hornsea Bridge station to the final terminus on the front.

It remained open until 9th. June 1912, when a new island platform opened to the west, serving both sets of branch trains and replacing both it and the old Sculcoates. The original bridge over the Hull, a single width one on which the double lines were guantletted, that is, interlaced within one another, was replaced by a swing structure in the NER house style in 1907, which still swings at the time of writing, as it carries a pedestrian right of way which must be expensive to maintain in the circumstances. Stepney station was where the East Dock branch crossed Beverley road, while Cemetery Gates lay at the crossing with Springbank, a busy place locally. Passenger traffic was unusually light for the area, so the powers-that-be, suspecting that the name was the cause, especially for those of advancing years, changed it to Botanic Gardens!

The Hornsea company soon felt the need for extra cash and went the same way as the H & H, selling out to the NER on 4th. January 1866, leaving much potential realised both en route, since hardly anywhere was developed by the lineside, or at the sea end, though Hornsea probably fared better in the end than did Withernsea, with smarter roads and better housing development round the stations; that at Hornsea Bridge served its own hinterland where the goods yard was situated. Both resorts catered for the businessman working in Hull, but Withernsea had, in addition, the crowds of East Hull trippers out for the day.

First attemps at reaching York

Although the Hull & Selby had an easy run over the level stretch of line along the Humber bank, and although the Bridlington branch was also flat, nevertheless the Wolds offered a challenge to be overcome in getting a line through to York, either via Beverley or from the main line at Brough. The former route was in fact being surveyed by the H & S in 1845 when George Hudson took a hand in that company's affairs, giving his approval to the completion of the scheme. Included in the package was a line from Selby to Market Weighton, and this and the York line were authorised on 18th. June 1846, with the latter line opened from York to Market Weighton only on 4th. October 1847, with the Selby branch to Market Weighton on 1st. August 1848. This put Market Weighton at the end of two converging branches at the point where the Wolds began and where, for the time being at least, the cash had simply run out. Both branches had opened at a total cost of £536,000, plus a few extra thousands to buy up three local canals. The line over hill to Beverley would be bleak and expensive, though not too steep, with no attractions on the way. Powers were granted to build the line on 13th. July 1849, but these lapsed and it was left to the NER to finish things off; the line was opened to passengers on 1st. May 1865. If was perhaps typical Yorkshire thrift which saw the York-Market Weighton branch reduced to a single line until the through route to Beverley was completed, the lines thus available being used to double the Leeds & Selby.

Not strictly to do with Hull, but Market Weighton had its 'cross' of railways completed by the opening of the line from there to Driffield on 18th. April 1890, which caused the doubling of the Selby-Market Weighton line from 1st. July 1890 and made available a new route for coast bound traffic from the industrial parts of the county, which in turn took these trains away from their passage round the outskirts of Hull. Enthorpe, on the new line, took some beating for isolation and lack of custom, situated miles from anywhere down a deep cutting. Kipling Cotes looked more civilised but fared little better on the Beverley line.

Strange Schemes

The Railway Mania, as it was called, reached its peak in the year 1845, when all kinds of schemes came up for air, gasped and were then drowned without trace. Any place of any size was to be linked to similar places up and down the country, while those schemes which had already been passed were imitated by parallel ones running nearby to stifle their chances of success. It was a good time for surveyors, accountants and speculators, much as nowadays, with hotels, corporate entertainment and golf courses mooted at every point where a motorway meets somewhere interesting. Soon, of course, the bubbles would burst, with empty pockets and sad faces all round. Hull was not excluded from the spree, nor indeed is it today. Below are the names of some of the lines projected, and is will be noted that one or two ideas are not far off the mark when the final railway topogaphy was established:

The Sheffield, Hull & Midland Direct (via Rotherham, Doncaster and Goole).

The Lincolnshire & Eastern Countries.

The Liverpool & Hull Direct (via Burnley & Leeds).

The Hull & Holyhead Direct.

The Northampton, Lincoln & Hull Direct.

The Hull, Malton & North Riding Union.

The York-Hull line was positive enough in the minds of the Y & NM directors, though what is of special interest to the reader was a branch suggested from Market Weighton to run south to Brough on the Hull & Selby, 'or such other point as might be deemed expedient'. In the event the idea was frightened off by the formation of a Railway Mania company, the Hull & Great North of England which blocked the scheme from the outset, though not before many words had been aired in various places. The Rev. Stillingfleet of South Cave had some well chosen phrases to ventilate on the subject of the great unwashed of Hull who would be likely to come out to his village on Sunday afternoons by the railway and soil the lanes with their uncouth behaviour. The subject of the line was raised again in 1847 by Mr. Egginton who referred to surveys made by the H & S and of the advantages of such a line, while the opposition on the part of local clergy and others continued. The scheme was revived in 1856 as the Hull & Market Weighton Railway Company, with Sir William Worsley of Hovingham Hall as chief shareholder. The advantages offered were that the line would shorten the journey to York by ten miles and avoid delays to passengers at Milford Junction. It was also claimed that the line would be dead level, a fact which is, however, hard to swallow, in view of its projected path through Brantingham and Drewton. The NER opposed the line, probably because it ran counter to the accepted lie of things from east to west, and was thus put in abeyance, the company meanwhile pressing ahead with the route through Cherry Burton to Beverley.

The Goole Branch

So far so good. With the line opened through the Wolds to York from Beverley much had been accomplished in sorting out traffic for that city and points north; note how there were rumblings of interest developing over the idea of a railway through the hills from the young coalfields of South Yorkshire. In this proposal we see again a burgeoning Hull & Barnsley idea allied to what actually transpired, for the earlier plan was for a line to leave a point in Hull near to North bridge, thence by way of Anlaby, Willerby, Swanland and running south to Melton and Elloughton to avoid much of the hilly terrain, Everthorpe, Hook and Goole to join the Lancashire & Yorkshire. A branch would run to Thorne to join the Manchester, Sheffield & Lincolnshire and the line to Doncaster. It does sound as if this route, if implemented, would have made for railway clutter on the north Humber bank, around Melton in particular, where there was not a great deal of flat land to house both lines as well as the road. There would also have been a branch for Soth Cave and Market Weighton, giving the route desired above to York and the north. Mc. Turk reckoned that the saving of ten miles by this route and of 15 to 20 miles to the south by the major route through Goole would greatly assist Hull in its role as a major coal shipping port and be a setback for Grimsby and Hartlepool, with links to five other companies into the bargain. Mention is made of the crossing of the Ouse at Goole, which would be performed by a 'substantial opening bridge'.

The L & Y promoted a line which would enter Hull alongside the existing H & S as did the MS & L company. An independent Hull, West Riding & Lancashire line was suggested, as well as one, unnamed, to run to Hull via Drewton. In 1860 Alderman Moss chaired the committee of the Hull & Doncaster Railway, a line of fifteen miles which would leave the H & S at Staddle thorpe and run via Goole to Thorne to join the MS & L, a relatively simple plan which would fulfill all the benefits of McTurk's earlier scheme. The NER was interested and pledged itself to promote the Bill again if it were thrown out of Parliament. The Bill did become law, however, on 23rd. July 1863 and, as is said nowadays, the rest is history. The NER came to terms with the competition and allowed running powers to the SYR (MS & L) between Thorne and Hull in exchange for powers from Thorne to Doncaster. The L & Y also enjoyed similar privileges from Goole to Hull in exchanges for powers between Nornanton and Barnsley. The line was opened on 30th. August 1869 and has played a prime role in Hull's commercial activities ever since, apart from odd hiccups when the swing bridge, one of the biggest in Europe, has been damaged by foreign ships which seem unable to aim correctly at the opening provided, in spite of an impressive warning display of paintwork and fairy lights. The bridge, known as Skelton, delayed the opening of the line because of the time taken to construct it. The centre swing span was 250 ft. long and ran on a 30 ft. turntable, weighing 670 tons. It was reached by one and four fixed girder supports, each 116 ft. long to form a total viaduct of 830 ft.

At this stage in developments life was fairly settled around Hull on the railway front, with the NER in command of what might be termed a benevolent monopoly. The MS & L was using its powers to promote Hull traffic and the L & Y quite content as long as its Goole interests were allowed to prosper. The Hull Dock Company was run by the Corporation, assisted by the three aforementioned railway concerns who had members on the board. The docks had come into being first of all with Queen's in 1778, followed by Humber in 1809, with Princes following in 1829. The Railway Dock followed in 1846, then came Victoria in 1850 and Albert in 1869. After this the NER had spent much money in developing sidings and storage facilities around the docks, while the Hull Dock Company constructed the William Wright and St. Andrew's docks in 1880 and 1883. A further dock was planned for Saltend away to the east of all this activity, for which powers had been given to construct a branch off the Withernsea line; however, Hull Corporation were so restrictive in their requirements here that the Bill, though successful, was dropped.

The gentlemen of Hull enjoyed an uneasy relationship with the NER, constantly suspecting that they were being short changed and overlooked in preference to other ports -Hartlepool has already been mentioned. In fairness, however, it must be that with the company, though a monopoly through no fault of its own, did its best with the lines of communication. It was no help that the MS & L was now pouring in traffic via the new access through Goole, which was in fact slowly choking the system in spite of a new and independent goods station at Kingston street, opened in 1873.

More schemes - across the Humber

Things came to a head in October 1872 when it became obvious that the facilities provided by the NER to deal with the railway traffic were hopelessly inadequate. Orders from places like Leeds were taking up to three weeks to deliver and much traffic was lost. Wagonloads of goods awaiting clearance stretched up to eight miles back along the line, while the NER was reluctant to accept grain consignments off the docks. Fish could no longer be dispatched as quickly as necessary for its fresh receipt at the other end. There were letters to the press, and almost as many meetings, at which the MS & L and L & Y were called upon to relieve the stranglehold which the NER was seeming to exert. On Friday, 1st. November 1872, in Hull Town Hall a sub-committee was formed to discuss the adoption of a new and independent line, the Hull, South & West Junction Railway. The capital for this would be £960,000 in ten shilling shares. Local worthies on the board of directors were Christopher Sykes MP of Brantinghamthorpe, Robert Jameson, Mayor of Hull, C. H. Wilson of Ganton Hall and Roland Winn of Appleby Hall, Brigg. The route was surveyed by John Fowler and began on the eastern side of Hull, passing round the town to Hessle and tunnelling under the river through chalk to Barton and striking south to the MS & L at Appleby, where connection was made with the Doncaster-Grimsby line. A branch would be laid from Keadby to the L & Y at Goole, thus anticipating the Axholme

Joint Railway of much later times. This was later added to by a spur from the MS & L at Barnby Dun to the L & Y at Askern. The length of the line with branches was to be about forty miles, while the tunnel, under shallow water, would be 1⅝ miles. The report was couched in glowing terms and claimed support from the influential among many wealthy parties up and down the country. Had the line been built, it would have made a great physical impact on places to the west of Hull; unfortunately it was defeated in the Lords due to the extent of the works needed for the tunnel. There had actually been a similar scheme mooted in 1865 by the GN, MS & L and GE companies, supported by Hull Corporation, for independent access to the town, the thinking this time being from the other end. The line would run from Bardney to Snelland on the MS & L, which would be used to the eastern curve at Barnetby, whence there would be a new line to Barton. From here a high level viaduct would carry traffic across to Hessle, where the new life would run alongside the H & S route into Hull. There were also ideas for a link with the new route of a Leeds, North Yorks. & Durham Railway from Hessle to Market Weighton, Wharram and Rillington. It all sounds now like a fantastic pipe dream, and the whole lot foundered most likely on the fearsome prospect of the railway bridge, a daunting one both visually and financially; the present road bridge might be expensive, but is certainly pleasing to the eye and elegant.

The incipient Hull & Barnsley

After all the above mentioned testing of the waters, as it were, it seemed that the time was at last right to float yet another independent railway company, this time one which would succeed where the others had foundered either through timing or impracticability. So it came to pass that the Hull, Barnsley & West Riding Junction Railway came into being at a meeting in the NER Station Hotel in Hull on 28th. May 1879. Its sponsors were two local men, Colonel Gerard Smith and Robert Galland, a banker and a solicitor. The line of route echoed that of the Hull & Barnsley Junction of 1845 and the Hull & West Riding Junction of 1862. The costs of £4 million included a new deep water dock for the export of coal. The Hull Dock Company supported the project and the Corporation gave £100,000, a somewhat modest amount and sold 126 acres of land to the company. These deals were hedged about with restrictions as to the selling or leasing of company property, and on joint working with anyone else.

The Hull Dock Company realised after a short time that there would soon be a competing dock in its vicinity and so actually opposed the passing of the H & BR Bill together with the NER, fearing for the effects upon its traffic and revenue. Parliament was to be swayed by the fact, among other things, that Hartlepool had good, new dock facilities of 200

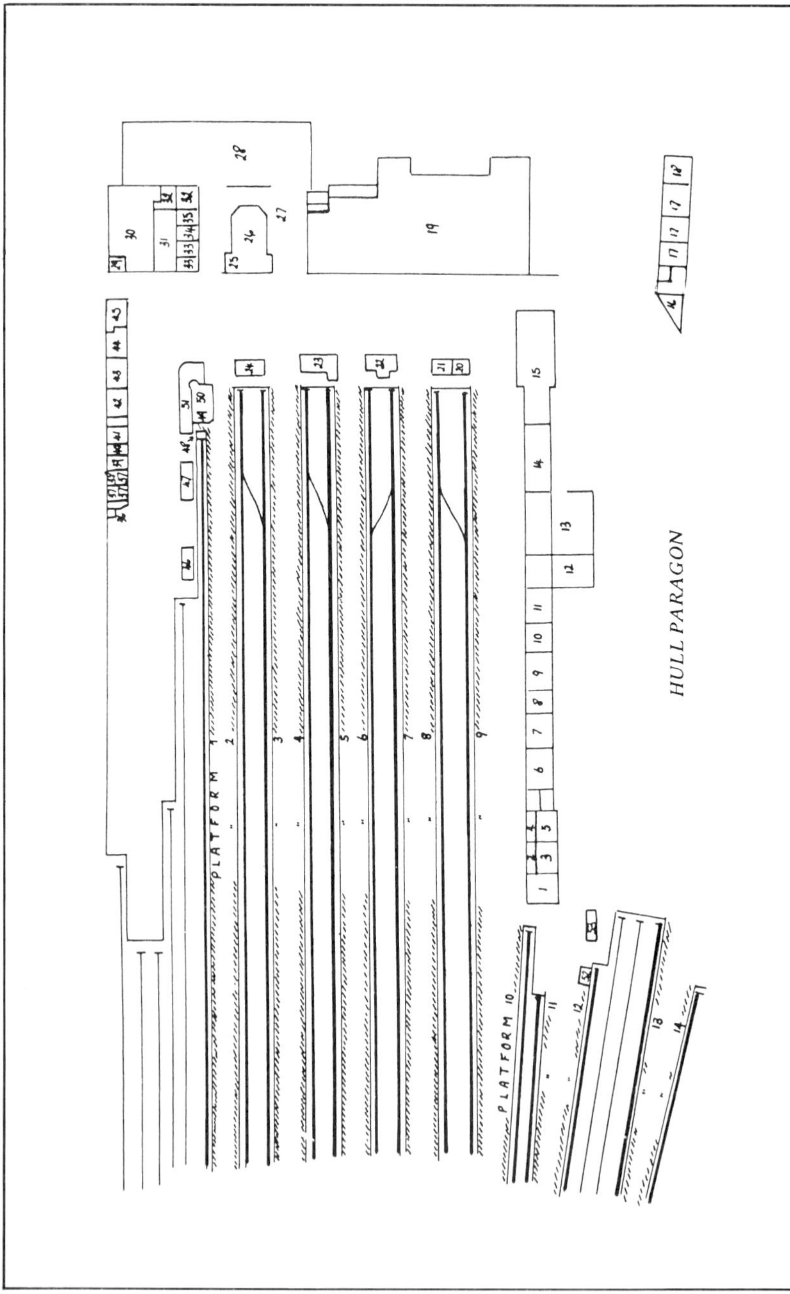

HULL PARAGON

Disposal of Offices at Hull Paragon Station before 1939

Key to the numbered plan, which is not to scale

1. Fish and Game store.
2. Oil store.
3. Lamp Room.
4. Coal store.
5. Foot warmers.
6. Guard's Room.
7. Gentlemen's Room.
8. Clerk's Lavatory.
9. General Room.
10. Ladies' Labatory.
11. Ladies Room.
12. Classroom.
13. Examination Room.
14. Abstract Office.
15. Parcels Office.
16. Yard.
17. Stock Room.
18. Garage.
19. Station Hotel.
20. Hairdressing (Gents.)
21. Gentlemen's Labatory.
22. Temperance Room.
23. Refreshment Room.
24. Gentlemen's Lavatory.
25. Excess Luggage.
26. Booking Office.
27. Booking Hall.
28. Covered way for taxis.
29. Lost Luggage.
30. Left Luggage.
31. Telegraph Office.
32. Station Master's Clerks.
33. Continental Agent.
34. Assistant Station Master.
35. Station Master.
36. W.C.'s.
37. Coal store.
38. Foot warmers.
39. Guard's Room.
40. Ladies' Lavatory.
41. District Engineer.
42. General Room.
43. Porters.
44. Emigrants' Luggage.
45. Foreman Porter.
46. Fish Office.
47. Milk Platform.
48. Ticket Collectors.
49. Lavatories.
50. Ladies' Room.
51. Tea Room.
52. Fish and Fruit Office.
53. Fish Stage.

acres of water and 150 acres of standage, compared to Hull's 114 acres of water and poorer facilities. Setting aside some discontent in the House of Lords, the Bill was passed on 26th. August 1880.

Construction of the new line was rapid, even though there were delays due to shortage of money, in fact Parliament took the unusual step of loaning £2½ million to supplement the £3 million available, so that, in effect the total cost was to be £1½ million in excess of the estimates. Alexandra Dock was filled on 21st. May 1885, being flooded with fresh water from the Holderness drain at 10 a.m. by Mrs. Smith, wife of the chairman. Later that day Mrs. Bohn, wife of the resident engineer, turned the last sod to mark the completion of the work. On 25th. May a special train was run to Stairfoot at the extreme end of the line, near Barnsley. Passengers included the contractors, Messrs. Luceas & Aird's foremen, who were given a chance to see the finished work. The journey from Alexandra Dock and back, with refreshments at the far end was completed without a hitch. On 28th. May more water was run into the new dock by Mrs. Fisher, wife of the deputy chairman, after which came a luncheon on the South Quay and a bevy of speeches. After all this followed the real entertainment, for the party repaired to a special train waiting alongside Hedon road, to be hauled by an 0-6-0 No. 14 for a run to the Ouse Bridge. The outfit was made up of five 4 wheelers and two brake vans, with departure set for 3.15 p.m. The 'Hull Daily Express' gave the following account on 29th. May 1885:

'Mr. Vincent Hill conducted the party and a start was made at about a quarter past three o'clock. The train proceeded without stoppage until Willerby was reached. The aspect of the town as presented from a higher level than railway travellers of the district have been accustomed to was remarked upon generally, and as the Wolds were approached the scenery was much admired. Proceeding westwards the immense cuttings in the hills were very noticeable and were a topic of conversation with those who had not previously seen the progress of the work. When just clearing the hill country in the vicinity of South Cave an accident occurred which detained the train for a considerable time. The engine, which had only been previously used a short time, was found to be temporarily defective and two contractor's engines were stopped on the line and brought into use for taking the train forward. Howden was reached in due course, and a stoppage was made to enable an inspection of the station and other works. A large number of town people were assembled to see the train-in fact villagers along the route from Hull had turned out at different points to see the novelty of a passenger train on the new line.

Ouse bridge was reached late in the afternoon and there the company alighted and inspected this fine piece of engineering work. It is generally regarded as one of the most beautiful of railway bridges, the ironwork being of that open and lattice construction which is much more acceptable than the solid sided bridges often met with on railways. The company assembled on the middle of the bridge and, while the refreshments were

The cabin on top of Willmington swing bridge. *C. T. Goode*

being served the machinery was set to work and the bridge swung several times. During the proceedings the Mayor called for Three Cheers for the success of the undertaking; cheers being heartily given, the Mayor leading. The return trip was then commenced, the train arriving at Cannon Street passenger station at about eight o' clock.'

Alexandra dock was opened officially to traffic on 16th. July 1885, with a ceremony attended by the customary junketing, poetry and fireworks at the Botanic Gardens, though not by the Archbishop of York who declined his invitation to attend.

The railway was opened for goods traffic on the 20th. and to passenger traffic on the 27th., the trains running to the terminus at Cannon Street, just north of the centre of Hull. Here was a temporary effort which, as most temporary things do, lasted the whole of the independent life of the line and which stood in for what might have been a palatial affair in Kingston Square that failed to materialise.

Overbridges were plentiful in the Hull area because the H & B had chosen to sit above roads and the NER below it. There were 35 within the town boundary. There were two swing bridges on the line, both of similar design by Shelford, the engineer. These were of lattice girder construction as opposed to the slab sided girder type favoured by the NER, a construction which certainly looked lighter, presented less wind resistance but was still, at 649 tons in the case of the Ouse bridge, on the heavy side. This bridge was 248 ft. at its swinging span and a little over 400 ft. with its run-up spans. The Hull bridge, which was on the goods line from Beverley Road Jc. to Alexandra Dock was, in contrast, a mere 131 ft. on its swing span. An interesting feature of the Ouse bridge was that, being pivotted centrally unlike most, it was in theory possible to keep rotating it like a roundabout, which may have happened with the guests at the opening day (above).

Just short of the junction with the main line at Sculcoates was the station of Beverley Road serving that thoroughfare and the larger houses round about in which several senior company officials resided. The line stayed high on embankment through its yards and past the locomotive shed at Springhead to reach Willerby station, then tackling the Wolds, first in a deep cutting of 83 ft. to Little Weighton station, and then by the Drewton tunnel of 2,116 yd. and two smaller versions, Sugar Loaf and Weedley, to reach South Cave. The line was solidly constructed with a staff who were fiercely proud of its reputation. However, troubles there were, and one of thses stemmed from the inconveniently sited station at Cannon Street which lay in a seedy part of the town, always redolent of linseed oil from the local paint works. Traffic was sparse on the passenger

Hull Bridge, carrying the H & B Alexandra Dock line. *C. T. Goode*

side, and coal movements grew only slowly, reaching their peak at the outbreak of the Great War, when they were effectively finished off. The major source of contention was the competition between the H & B, NER and Hull Dock Company, all of whom reduced dock charges, a ruinous practice by the two smaller concerns. The L & Y, hitherto dormant in the matter of running powers to the town, had seen the fur flying and now joined the MS & L in seeking Hull traffic. A spur on the east side of Hull which would have allowed the NER access to Alexandra Dock remained unfinished after 1887, and nothing futher was done during the lives of the separate companies.

Dock developments

The H & B found itself heavily in debt and appealed to its lifeline at Cudworth, the Midland Railway for help. The Midland had been able to provide the quickest route between the Midlands and Hull via this outpost at the extremity of the H & B, and leapt at the thought of amalgamation with such an ambitious little railway. The coal owners of South Yorkshire, however, who had enjoyed cheap rates, thought differently, while the Hull Corporation, who had placed restrictions on the leasing or taking over of the line without their consent, fumed on the sidelines. Thus another scheme foundered and the NER was saved from the spectre of little red engines breezing about over their heads. The Corporation invoked an Act of 1861 which allowed them to compel the Dock Company to form a Dock Trust to administer the whole of Hull's docks, an idea which would settle the H & B's debts and please the Dock Company by appropriating Alexandra Dock, making the H & B the preferred route into the city. The H & B opposed the idea, fearing the loss of its most valuable property, as did, surprisingly enough, the Dock Company. In 1889 the latter presented A Bill to cover a new working arrangement with the NER, one which was respected by Parliament as it was not likely to result in any improvements of the docks. Better accommodation was waiting for the fishing fleet, now with bigger, steam powered vessels which devoured copious supplies of coal, while deep water facilities were needed, including a new entrance to Albert Dock.

What was obviously needed was a new deep water dock which the H & B was prepared to finance, though at the cost of not proceeding with other improvements. In1891 and again in 1893 they suggested a take-over of the Hull Dock Company, the second time agreeing with the H & B not to undertake any further rounds of charge-cutting. The NER even got round to agreeing with the H & B that any new dock should be built to the east of Alexandra Dock on vacant land owned by the H & B and built as a joint venture by both of them. Having witnessed a rapport of sorts between the two companies, the NER submitted a new Bill for the acquistion of the Dock Company, which received Royal assent on 24th. August 1893. Through this the NER took over eight docks, various basins and 100 acres of water, plus 40 acres of timber ponds at a total cost of £2¼ million. The Corporation looked askance at this manoeuvring, not liking the coinciding of H & B and NER interests which might raise dock charges to an unrealistic level, though some of the H & B directors felt that the opposite would happen once the Dock Company had lost its position as arbiter in the matter. Really the NER was quite reasonable in its conduct towards the port of Hull, and after the tussle of the take-over in the docks had died down to some extent, the company took steps to improve the lot of the fishing trade, building a ten acre basin with attendant jetties at St. Andrew's Dock for trawlers in 1894. In 1906 the Riverside Quay was opened by the NER to handle fruit and vegetables, also a service for passengers worked jointly with the L & Y between Hull and the continent.

More would have been done in the matter of deep water docks had it not been for the unwillingness of the H & B to prejudice their monopoly embodied in the Alexandra Dock. Amalgamation between the two railway companies was proposed for a second time, and again various factions, H & B shareholders, the Chamber of Commerce and others, objected, fearful of what an NER monopoly could mean. They could offer nothing

Hessle station in NE days. The tank engine and brake is probably delivering to the signal box. *Heyday Publishing Company*

Stopping train leaving Ferriby for Selby, D17 4.4.0 No. 1632. *T. Rounthwaite*

that was acceptable, and even the offer, in 1897 to construct a new river wall and various dock improvements was rejected by groups including the Aire & Calder navigation on the grounds that they would most likely interfere with Humber shipping movements. In 1898 the NER sought permission to extend Victoria Dock eastwards with greater storage for timber and sidings for coal shipment. This, too, was rejected, the Corporation rather pettishly suggesting that the NER might be better employed in replacing its level crossings by overbridges.

A light was now in sight with the 1893 agreement to build a new joint dock to the east of Alexandra Dock, with mutual running powers where required round Hull, including the passenger stations. It goes without saying that the Corporation objected, but this time common sense prevailed; they were overruled and the Joint Dock Act was passed in 1900. It took fifteen years before King George V could come to the city and open the dock on 26th. June 1914, a magnificent addition to the port and offering two large graving docks and total water area of 53 acres. Along with this came the jointly owned oil jetty at Saltend, east of the dock and extending some 1,500 ft. into the Humber. Possibly because the world was becoming more sophisticated and used to state events, and because reporters now found more to write about, the opening ceremony for the Joint Dock was restrained, without the spectacle which had

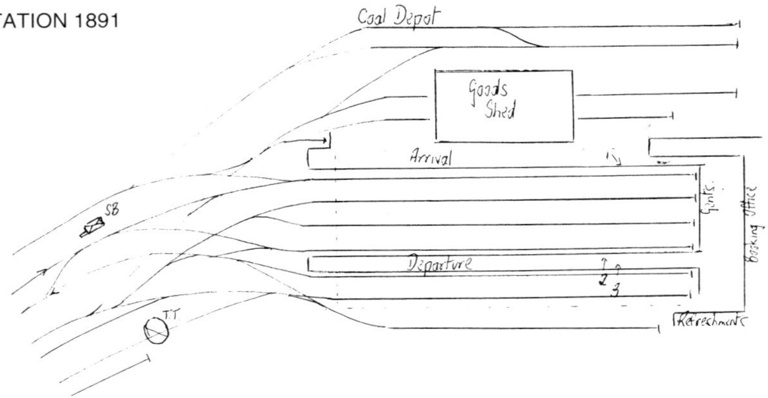

CANNON STREET STATION 1891

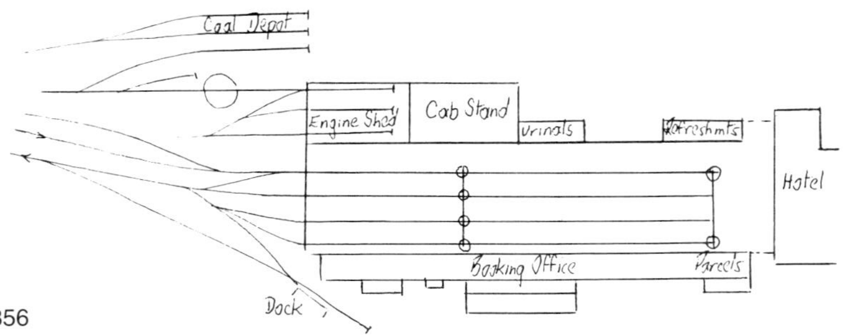

PARAGON STATION 1856

attended the opening of Alexandra Dock. As well as a personal appearance by the King, a commemorative medal and brochure with colour prints appeared, headed by the new badge for the Joint Committee.

Dairycoates yards and the 'straight line'

The old Hull & Selby line along the Humber bank had developed logically over the years, as befitted the entry to one of the largest ports in the country, with double track initially, though by 1890 there were four tracks from west of Brough, probably put in at about the same time as the halt at Broomfleet. Hessle station had its main approach from the southern side, while Ferriby was a simple affair with a siding for each direction and a small level crossing box. Between here and Hessle were chalk pits and whiting mills with their own railways which burrowed beneath the line and were unconnected with it. By 1928 Hessle Quarry signal box had established itself on the north side of the line, with sidings connected to the main line, a private railway with engine shed and a stone crushing mill. East of Hessle were large ranges of coal sidings at Dairycoates between the lines which ran to Paragon station and the old route along the river bank to Manor House. In 1909 the Inward and Mineral Haven and East signal boxes appeared. Later there was an extension called Priory Yard, while on the Up or south side of the main line lay Outward Yard, used for the making up of fast goods services.

At Dairycoates was the locomotive depot and sidings were sandwiched in wherever possible, flanking running lines and even as far as the level crossing gates at Hessle Road. The old 'straight line' up from here to Cottingham had been superseded by the opening of Paragon station many years before, to be used only for excursions not stopping in Hull, and goods services. All this, too dwindled on the opening of the line from Market Weighton to Driffield which provided a new way of reaching Bridlington from Selby. A station existed at Newington crossing, where the 'Straight line' crossed Anlaby road; it was a wooden affair of narrow platforms squashed up against a tram depot at one side. For many years this was used to cope with excursion trains visiting the nearby fair each October, when trains would arrive from the north to set down and run empty to Dairycoates for stabling, those from the south running on to Beverley or Driffield for similar hospitality. The story goes that, around 1896 the wife of the local timber merchant Mr. Jameson was due to return to Hull in delicate health and that, as they lived nearby, it was asked whether she might leave the train at Newington. The NER agreed, provided that Mr. Jameson erect a station using his own men and materials at no cost to the company.

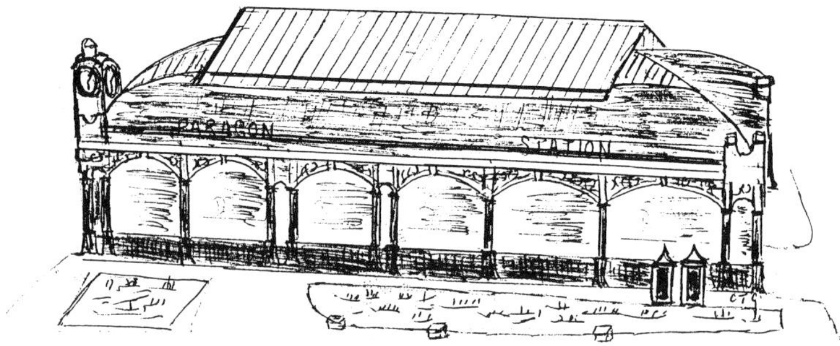

The canopy over the forecourt at Paragon station

Paragon station

There were no intermediate stations on the line into Paragon station, only five level crossings initially to enliven the run in. The original station was designed by G. T. Andrews and covered 2 ½ acres on the south side of the lines, running alongside Anlaby road, pillared and imposing and served by a gated yard from the road. The building still serves as staff quarters and a parcels office. Somewhat battered by wind and weather it is almost hidden from view by intrusive buildings adjacent to the road. The enlarged station of 1904 had extra platforms within the overall roof on the south side and a new booking hall alongside the frontage of the Station Hotel, facing Paragon street. The new entrance was set back a short distance to allow the movement of cabs and other unloading vehicles. This was covered by an open iron canopy with a clock at its southern end. The canopy went in 1962, while the booking hall survives externally in its original condition. On leaving the booking office the station proper could be reached, its roof of five spans covering nine main platforms, of which the largest was almost 800 ft. The total number of platforms was fourteen, with the extras lying outside the main layout, No. 10 as a recessed section of No. 9 and suitable for short trains or railcars, as were Nos. 11 and 12 which often stood in as goods platforms. Nos. 13 and 14 were long excursion platforms for extra and relief services.

Looking towards Hessle Road Jc. from Dairycoates. The Neptune St. branch crosses Hessle Road and the NE lines. *Coll: C. T. Goode*

The nature of traffic may be conveyed by the use to which the twelve booking office windows, each in carved oak panelling surrounded by tiling, were put; Nos. 1-4 were on the south side, 6-7 facing the street, 5 and 8 on the angles and the rest on the north side.

Eventually those on the north side fell out of use, but below is how they were employed round about 1930:

1. Goole and intermediate stations. H & B line
2. Thorne, Doncaster, Sheffield.
3. Selby, Leeds, York.
4. Short journeys, Hessle etc.
5. Hornsea, Withernsea.
6. Thousand Mile tickets.
7. Advance bookings.
8. General.
9. Enquiries after hours.
10. York via Market Weighton.
11. Bridlington, Scarborough.
12. Seasons, Party bookings.

In 1929 one million passengers were booked in the year with, no doubt, a similar number of arrivals. Up to 170 trains departed daily, plus extras on Saturdays and holiday periods. Hull & Barnsley line trains used No. 1 platform, while the prime London trains used No. 9.

The engine sheds

As was the case with railways and many other matters during the pre 1914 period, great improvements were afoot, and as well as activities along the Humber bank, a new layout was put in hand at Wilmington in 1910, together with a new swing bridge. The first engine shed opened at Dairycoates, the name of the farm on the site (in two words) in 1863, with a new shed coming along in 1915, comprising six roundhouses and a straight shed. In 1923 a total of 150 engines was based there. Botanic Gardens, a sub-shed, was nearer the passenger station and dealt with guest arrivals and passenger workings, home to 47 engines at about the same period. Its history is part of that of the original shed at Paragon station, erected on the north side in 1848, extended in 1867 and 1876. In 1904 it was transferred round to Botanic Gardens in readiness for the station extensions.

In the roundhouses at Dairycoates the turntables were three of 50 ft. and three of 60 ft. in diameter, with 130 radiating 'spokes on which to stand engines. There was the usual range of repair shops and messing facilities for the staff. The mechanical coaling stage was brought into use in March 1916 and was one of the largest in the country. Coal was unloaded into an underground hopper, then crushed to the correct size and raised to places ready for use by up to four engines at a time, which could also be watered simultaneously. Water was pumped for use at the depot from a treatment station which was set in the yard at Hessle, and the hum of the machinery was a familiar experience there, adding to the tones of the block bells and clash of levers in the station signal box.

The Hull & Barnsley soldiered on for a few more years after the Great War before being absorbed into the old adversary, the NER, on 1st. April 1922, just a year before the melting pot of Grouping, when many more famous initials passed into oblivion. The first thing done by the NER was to order the discontinuation of further major repairs at Springhead works, the closure of part of them and the consequent loss of jobs, unless men chose transfer to Darlington, not a popular move in those days or indeed at any time. The H & B engines were run down and, indeed, in many cases no boiler repairs had been done since the engines had been purchased. Once the NER had taken over the company, a plan of replacement was undertaken, and in the case of the large 0-8-0 goods engines a new type of domed boiler was fitted, fifteen in all by Darlington to give the engines life up to 1931. New NER numbers beginning with a 3 were given to ex H & B engines, which was confusing, especially as they were again renumbered two years later to conform with the LNER pattern. The 4-4-0s also sported green livery for a time, which must have jarred a little with the older enginemen!

The whole site at Springhead occupied some 20 acres originally, with the shed set in a 'green field' site with locomotive, carriage and wagon works added from 1890, complete with a 60 ft. chimney, erecting shop and carriage shed. The sheds were extended in 1907 and a coaling stage was brought into use in mid 1908. All this activity was to the north of the main line, with the loco. repair shops to the north of the running shed and carriage and wagon shops to the north west. At the time of the take over in 1922, some 1,220 men were employed at Springhead. After 1924 sufficient gear was left to maintain locomotives in the Hull area, including Dairycoates and Botanic Gardens, while the practice grew of using Springhead to store locomotives when they were not required for duties, either when fresh ex works, or redundant. In 1922 43 Hull & Barnsley engines were scrapped by the NER.

The line to Beverley

The exit from Paragon station was most impressive, with three lines of route, to Staddlethorpe, to Bridlington and the perverse one to Holderness, off in the wrong direction, all running together as far as West Parade signal box, where they resolved themselves. There were originally cabins at Paragon station itself, Park Street, just outside and West Parade, the latter a hefty cabin which had the task of sorting things out into its correct destination. The centre of the three routes here led out to Cottingham, Beverley and Bridlington, passing almost immediately over Victoria Crossing where the line bisected a spur from the Staddlethorpe line to the Botanic Gardens line, after which came the carriage sheds on the left side and Walton Street crossing, supervised by a cantilevered signal box of similar pattern to that found at Grosmont, but smaller. This crossing had an early form of low level gates which ran on rubber wheels and were motor worked. Walton Street controlled the lower end of the spur down from the H & B at Springbank, put in when that company's traffic was re-routed into Paragon station in 1924. Beyond here the line swings round beneath the H & B to pass the Ideal Boiler Works, originally American Radiator Company, which had a siding on the right hand side, to reach Cottingham South Jc. at the point where the old Manor House route to Bridlington, the 'straight line' came in. For years the signal box here had a pronounced backwards lean, which must have caused problems with the signalman's teamaking. The name was interesting, as Cottingham lay still a mile or two from here. The station at Cottingham was perhaps typical NER in style, with low buildings on the west side and a reasonable waiting shed on the other. The yard lay beyond, also on the west side. South of the station was the little crossing box, Thwaite Gates, a tongue twister and one of the jaunty wooden cabins beloved of the NER-one still exists at Cave, near Broomfleet, while the real business of the station was controlled by Cottingham North signal box, which also handled the busy and complex road crossing at the north end. When the future of the line lay in the balance in the 1960s, the station was given a

D49 No. 62772 'The Sinnington' runs into Hull over Anlaby Road crossing.
C. T. Goode

gleaming new set of gas lamps, probably in a defiant gesture by someone or other.

From here the line passes into highly valuable market gardening country, with a siding for the waterworks on the Down side, a hush-hush installation, also on the Down side which was probably a petrol area for planes, with a small signal box at Cottingham Moor and level crossing over a remote country lane at Beverley Parks signal box, this at two miles from Cottingham. The author remembers the horrible fascination of sitting looking forward in the then new diesel multiple unit as the driver, distracted by something down in his compartment, passed the stop signal here and went through the gates. Fortunately there was no road traffic, only a great deal of unpleasant language immediately afterwards. Beverley station came at 1 mile 998 yd. futher on, preceded by a busy road crossing at Flemingate, then the Station cabin and station proper. This was, and still is, a fine example of Y & NM architecture, with its overall roof now renewed, and it always surprises that reference is hardly ever made in local historical guides, in spite of its size and obvious interest. The restoration is well done and worth a visit. There were eight such premises in the area, at Bridlington, Driffield, Market Weighton, Rillington, Filey, Malton and Pocklington. The last three retain their roofs, together with Beverley. Pocklington has become a gymnasium. The best must have been Rillington, on the York-Scarborough line, built for some reason with an overall roof which was removed in 1955. The sight and sound of express trains at full speed whooshing along beneath must have been worth experiencing. There was a decent sized goods yard at Beverley on the left side, and a long Up relief line of 733 yd. from Beverley North signal box which was allowed latterly to fall into disuse until a spell of very hot weather buckled it in a dramatic way and removal was necessary. Its exit was controlled by a primitive cross bar signal. An intermediate signal box was Cherry Tree, working another level crossing.

From Beverley North the branch to York led off to the north west.

The line to Brough

One of the noticeable features of railway landscape in the Hull area, indeed in any place of importance served by the NER were its masses of signals, especially the huge and weighty latticework gantries with posts carrying arms of different sizes; or there would be wooden specimens with huge finials and lead alloy spikes, often bracketed or performing aerobatics off the sides of warehouses and walls. This was the apparent policy of one particular S & T Engineer, Mr. Hurst, who evolved the system of signalling with small repeater signals, backing and calling-on signals, in fact signals to cover every possible eventuality, with each arm working in a slot in the post which carried it. Surprising it was that there were hardly any difficulties in operating the system because of snow choking up the slots. Whereas many companies favoured one distant signal as a warning before a junction, Hurst had a separate arm for each route, thus adding to the melee and possible confusion for 'foreign' crews of engines from other areas. So it was that the way out of Paragon was lined with a triumphal arch of signals. The level crossing had a busy road and tram lines to contend with; there was an auxiliary gateman in a hut at the roadside to help move the gates, which were long ones, to and fro and shorten the delays. Mercifully, however, someone did have the sense to put the crossover by which engines off trains at Paragon could reverse round the triangle over Victoria Crossing short of the gates, to save extra misery for road users. There were St. George's Road and Chalk Lane (Hawthorn Avenue) cabins, both level crossings and little wooden greenhouses, and Hessle Road signal box and level crossing within just one mile of Anlaby Road. This was probably the worst (or most interesting) crossing on the line, with a busy road, cramped conditions beneath a large bowstring girder bridge carrying the H & B branch to Neptune street, a tram route, a junction on the north side where the 'straight' line left and, at the south side, sidings and entry to the dockland area and the loco. depot at Dairycoates. No less than eight lines curved round east to Dairycoates East Jc., a massive cabin which controlled one end of the shed and lines along to Billingsgate Goods and Albert Dock West Jc.

Round to the west from Hessle Road a yard of fifteen roads hugged the passenger lines on their south side as they ran to Hessle East Jc., while south of this complex a further pair of lines ran to Dairycoates West Jc., another large signal box with its bay window for observation purposes serving the vast Outward yard with its spread of 41 sidings, all through ones, and a block of 32 (or thereabouts) running to dead-ends at Coal Sidings East Jc., with the old Hull & Selby approach lines thrown off into various sidings and small yards to make the topgraphy interesting as far as Coal Sidings West Jc., after which the whole filigree was tied into a neat knot to emerge at Hessle East. Odd wagons were lost from time to time in such locations, and lists were circulated of their numbers and 'chasers' employed to seek them out. One pities the young signal lad sent to his first post to a cabin in the midst of all this activity; it would be imperative to get the name of the box firmly fixed in his head! The two Coal Sidings boxes were more than likely not worked under absolute block regulations, having enough to do managing the complicated yard movements. The crunch was in the form of a timber yard and a further set of ten through lines nearby, set south of all this activity down by the edge of the Humber, the whole linked up at the Hessle end.

A scene not to be repeated! B1 4.6.0 No. 61276 awaits departure on the 12.12 p.m. to York in Hull Paragon. Alongside is a diesel service for Withernsea. C. T. Goode

So far there has been no mention of activity to the north of the main lines east of Hessle, on the land adjacent to Hessle road. Here the inward goods traffic for Hull had been handled for years in a small yard of nine sidings with a shunting neck capable of holding a mere 27 wagons, hardly sufficient for the number of docks and depots, plus other branch lines from Hull. This also meant that much traffic had to be handled on to other yards for secondary sorting.

New Inward Yard

On 9th. December 1935 a new inward of 30 sidings and six reception roads, fully mechanised, was opened. Here wagons could be placed into the correct road for direct forwarding to wherever required, though additionally there was a small flat yard of six through sidings for marshalling branch line traffic into station order for pick-up trains. The yard followed the pattern found at Whitemoor (near March) and Hamm in Germany, handling traffic from all directions, except H & B vehicles.

The reception lines could each hold up to 100 wagons and were reached from Hessle Haven signal box which also controlled the entrance to Priory Yard alongside. Trains from the east had access along a pair of running lines from Dairycoates West. Once the train engine had been detached from its load, the hump engine would reach it along its own line and propel it slowly over the hump of 1 in 18 to be 'cut' into different sidings as required, the shunter noting what was to be done, notifying the control tower and uncoupling at the right time. To enable the hump engine to move at the correct speed, a three position colour light was installed to inform the crew, as well as electric bells for use in fog. From the hump the detached wagons ran down the 1 in 50 into one of the four fans of 7, 8, 8 and 7 sidings to be slowed as required, often in a cloud of rust by one of the four Fröhlich retarders acting on their wheels, worked by hydraulic power under the hand of the brakesman. The points were also worked hydraulically from buttons on the panel in the control tower. The 30 sidings totalled some 24½ miles of track and funnelled newly formed trains into four departure roads to await release by the signalman at Dairycoates West. Most of the work of the yard was done between midnight and ten a.m. each day, and up to 3,000 wagons could be handled in 24 hours. The whole site was very avant-garde with overtones of Whitemoor and more than a passing hint of Teutonic efficiency.

The last remarks put one in mind of the modernisation which took place at Paragon station at about the same time, when two large signal boxes, both themselves modern with power signalling, were replaced by one new signal box on 24th. April 1938. These were the station signal box and Park Street, both mustering together 322 miniature levers with power for

A fine display of carriages on the left, plus a neat row of East Yorkshire bus roofs with white stripes as B1 No. 1306 leaves Paragon with the "Yorkshire Pullman".
C. T. Goode

operating the points, mechanical interlocking of levers and electro-pneumatic signalling. This system was replaced by one housed on the south side of the station and which virtually copied that installed at Leeds City a year previosly in 1937. In this the principle of route relay interlocking was used, whereby thumb switches on the diagram corresponded with the signals and points, and reversal of key switches can set up a route along the diagram for any particular train, provided that all is clear. At Hull the switches were in fact off the diagram and below it, though the operation was the same. Here there are 32 running signals, 18 having route indicators. and 56 subsidiary signals, while up to 230 routes were available. For movement of individual points if needed, a further 48 thumb switches were sited in a row below the diagram itself. Needless to say, the skyline was a lot clearer and denuded, once the old gantries of arms were removed, with just five large bracket posts made from old Shildon and Newport electric line supports in the shops at Hull manning the station run in. The actual station area was remarkably uncluttered.

Perhaps not untypical of the region, the large cabin at West Parade, which played a large part in the running of the train service in and out, was left unaltered with its large gantry and over 100 mechanical levers. It survived in reduced form until the 1970s.

A natural buoyancy in the growth of trade during the Edwardian period caused a quadrupling of the trackwork out as far as Staddlethorpe Jc., where the Doncaster branch came in, with the slow lines added to the outer sides of the existing rails. This meant a new station at Hessle with the approach now at the north side and an interesting set of buildings attached to the existing premises which were now left some way to the east. Hessle chalk quarry was developed below Hesslewood House and had an signal box linking it with the running lines, eccentrically in that there was, until closure, a turnout straight into the yard off the Up main line only, with a slip off this to the Down slow. Only the NER could get away with such a dubious practice. The several chalk pits continued to work independently of the railway, while the block was split up by cabins at various times, one being Swanland. Ferriby reached its final form, losing its level crossing and cabin and gaining a platform based signal box as at Hessle, set on the south side most conveniently for enthusiast and signalman alike. Between here and Brough developments took place around Melton Lane signal box and level crossing with the arrival of a cement and smelting works. An unadvertised halt appeared here at Melton in 1920 at which one train each way was due to stop daily, though more of then did seem to do so, if memory serves rightly. There was a crossing box known as Welton, too far away to work a ground frame at the outlet to the cement sidings at Melton in the Up Slow, before Brough was

Willerby station looking east. *M. Haddon*

Ex H & B 0.6.2T No. 2415 on a trip working near Ella Street. *T. Rounthwaite*

reached at 10½ miles from Hull. Brough was, in its heyday, quite an important place with turn-round trains to serve the locally imported workforce at the aircraft factory. Originally with two tracks only, came a level crossing, then sidings on the north side of the station as well as a yard on the south side, a gasworks (unconnected) at the west end beyond the road bridge across the centre of the station with signal box below it on the southern platform on its east side. To the west the formation took on slow lines, making the start of four tracks. On widening these were carried eastwards through the old layout, while new island platforms were built slightly east of the originals. There were new signal boxes at Brough East by the level crossing and Brough West east of the road bridge. There were also links to the gasworks and also to the timber yard opposite on the south side. New single storey station buildings were built north of the station away from the lines and adjacent to the original buildings, which have survived in various altered forms.

Alexandra Dock to Springhead

The Hull & Barnsley was quite a different line from the NER, a quieter, more of a boy's toy railway with its modest run of track coming in at high level over the roods, its signals which were wooden, solid and well painted, the nearest thing that one could get to the old Hornby 'O' gauge No. 2 variety with the arms of the posts, not within them and a pervading impression that the staff were playing at trains, moving rolling stock about to please themselves, as there were precious few passengers about, especially at Cannon Street.

When directions are mentioned, it is always Down to Hull and Up to Cudworth, a little perverse, seeing that Hull was the main attraction for the company. The main line proper began at the H & B and NER Joint King George Dock signal box, where many sidings were to be found, though mile posts were always reckoned from Alexandra Dock. The line was joint to Holderness Drain South signal box, from where the H & B proper began. Both companies ran at the side of Alexandra Dock, then joined up at Holderness Drain South to run parallel along Hedon road and crossing it by a bridge near to the entrance to Alexandra Dock. Alexandra Dock signal box was the largest on the system and controlled the various attendant sidings around the dock, as well as the line to the station which handled the emigrant traffic. From the double track across Hedon road there was, firstly, a double track off left leading off parallel with Hedon road towards the Graving docks which shed a few sidings, mostly through lines with spurs to coal hoists, warehouses and timber yards. The central double lines went south east, directly to the dockside warehouses and the

Hull Cannon St. in 1932 devoid of adverts, signs and hoardings. *Real Photos*

Little Weighton station. C. T. Goode

large signal box was within the fork of the two routes at this point; then, at the signal box a third double track curved south to more timber yards and the Alexandra Dock station. This was a simple affair with the main admin. buildings on the east side and a run-round facility for arriving engines on to a turntable line alongside. The station here was probably not used a great deal (see later references). The engine shed on the dock site was situated about as far from the station as could possibly be achieved, right at the eastern end of things, a two road affair which eventually disintegrated, leaving its occupants out in the open air.

From Alexandra Dock the line was now in position on embankment, firstly joined by a line up from the NER branch to King George Dock at Bridges Jc. This lay on the north side of the line and was presumably named after two overbridges carrying the lines over, opening in May 1914, then closing in 1917, open again on 2nd. March 1924 to 5th. June of that year, reopening September 1927 to 1931, finally opening in December 1941 and closing finally on a unspecified date.

Further round at a rather busy spot where the line passed over the Sutton drain and the Hornsea branch was Burleigh Street signal box, on the Down side a little way east of its yard on the opposite side which was entered by a facing connection in true NER fashion to meander into the works of the British Extraction Company. Actually a spur was planned here to join up with the NER at Wilmington station, but nothing was completed-this probably explains the odd signalling and facing point. Burleigh Street box opened in 1896 and the goods depot there dealt with general merchandise and coal. It was affiliated to Sculcoates (q.v.).

The crossing of the river Hull was made by a swing bridge of 131 ft., the combined signal box, engine pumphouse and hydraulic accumulator tower on the east bank Down side. The span was lattice bowstring and was designed by Mr. Shelford after a trip to France and Germany and built by Messrs. Handyside of Derby. There was a thirteen lever frame to work

A rare shot of an old H & B 2.4.0, most likely near Cannon St. signal box. John Hudson is the engine driver, right, with Walter Kirkwood, his fieman, on the centre.
R. Heathcote

things, with three spare levers. Once over the river, the area of Sculcoates was reached, with an extensive goods yard on the Up side, while on the Down, adjacent to the signal box a siding went off to serve the British Gas Company Works. The yard was an important one, employing up to 22 clerks by 1919, in offices and the large goods shed. Private sidings were put in and leased to various firms, notably the Hull Corporation Electricity Depot and Messrs. Blundell, Spence the paint makers, who had a large works to the south. The signal box had thirty levers and the entry to the goods yard was worked as a double line junction. Some 470 yd. west was Beverley Road Jc., the point where the passenger line from the terminus at Cannon Street came in. It was eventually decided to dispense with the block post situated just east of the road bridge and, from 9th. June 1936 a ground frame was put in, worked from Sculcoates. Quite a come-down for the line. The road bridge over Beverley road was specially finished as an iron fence supported by brackets and a bold circular panel on the spandrels, the latter ornamented with fish scales and the company emblem in the centre. The bridge over Newland avenue also had a simpler, decorated wooden parapet. All this elaboration was sadly seen off during the last major war.

Cannon Street

Cannon Street station was 1,625 yd. down a branch line from Beverley Road Jc. and was not what the company had in mind for a terminus. Their sights were set on something more palatial nearer to the centre of commerce; instead they settled for the site destined for the carriage sheds, as the cost of the solidly built wayside stations had absorbed most of the cash available for the purpose. The approach was difficult, through a poor part of the city shared by St. Paul's church and a couple of public houses. As it was, the passenger facilities were served by mean wooden buildings housing, as one looked from the road, a telegraph office, booking office, waiting rooms, inspectors' office and station master's office. Inside, down on the left were the refreshment rooms, in the centre was a bookstall and down the right hand side rooms for porters, guards and, nearest, parcels. It was an eery experience to visit the station in 1948 and find the refreshment rooms still there after almost a quarter of a century, locked with all its paraphernalia of urns, cups and the rest still on view inside. One could hardly imagine such items lasting in place for a fraction of the time nowadays! There were three platforms covered by an overall roof; the right hand one, No. 1 was the arrival which had also a long goods platform as its outer face. Between it and Nos. 2 and 3 which were each side of one island were two carriage sidings, while on the west side of No. 3 were two more lines. No. 3 could only handle departures, due to the pointwork. There was a carriage shed on the east side and a large goods yard on the other, the signal box of 35 levers being in the middle of things. This was replaced by a ground frame in 1924, and the cabin was still standing in 1948.

From the flatness of the station area came a twelve chain rise at 1 in 50 up to the embankment and the bridge over the Hornsea/Withernsea branch, curving round to reach Beverley Road station, a gaunt Victorian horror of a building on the south side of the line with one of the perky H & B

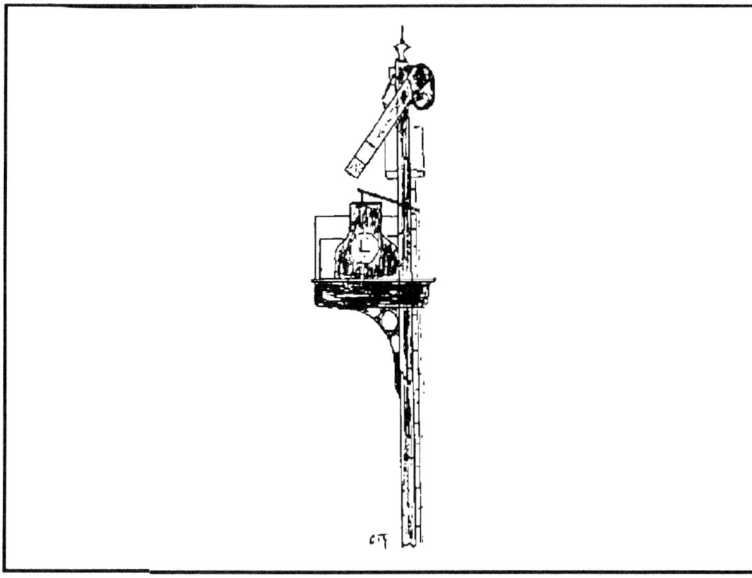

Reception signal at Locomotive Jc.

waiting sheds to relieve the gloom on the other. The building would have been softened in appearance when new, as it had a glass awning around it like a ballerina's skirt, no doubt to encourage the beau monde of the large houses nearby. Matthew Stirling, the mechanical engineer who lived nearby used the station to visit Springhead works, travelling in his personal saloon to do so.

Beverley Road station was virtually at the junction; in fact the original plans had the site for it to the west of the roadway on the main line. Along from here to the west Ella Street goods and coal yard, a small affair worked by a signal box of thirteen levers on the Up side, opened in 1906 and closed on 5th. October 1937, to be replaced by a ground frame controlled by Springbank North some 1 mile 370 yd. away. Between, the two lines crossed Chanterlands avenue by a bridge which was one of two replaced by a new one in 1923, having room for three tracks, in this instance to accommodate the extension of one of the sidings by 71 chains down to the National Radiator Works opened in 1906 and the National Wool sheds to the east. The latter were 18 ex Ministry of Munitions structures placed together around 1921, covering some nine acres and served four dead end sidings reached by a reverse shunt out of the running line. Activities do not seem to have lasted long, with four wool sales held in 1921. The sheds were disused by 1928. The National Radiator Company had access to its sidings from both the H & B and NER and had its own locomotive, a small Peckett 0-4-0 saddle tank of 1906 which worked both into Ella street yard and the NER sidings at Cottingham South. The engine ran over the H & B to Springhead from time to time when servicing was required.

Approaching Springbank North, trains had a choice of routes, namely straight ahead for Locomotive Jc. along the main line, centre leftwards into goods yards at Springbank West or left round to South box and Neptune Street. This was all heralded by three fine distant signals on a crossbar post, of which the NER would have been proud, then by high home signals with distants for the two branches below. The latter assembly lasted well into BR days, only spoilt by the NE practice of replacing part of a set of signals at a given site with NER style components, resulting here in the right hand post and arm being a slotted signal, the rest remaining H & B originals. The original signal box went as well, on 29th. June 1924 when the spur from here down to Walton Street, by which passenger services could reach Paragon station along the Bridlington line, was opened. It had 30 levers which were insufficient to cope with an extra junction; a new cabin with 45 levers was opened as replacement for the original, which was on the opposite side of the line.

Pursuing the lines through the yards, there were Up and Down goods lines to which came, firstly, a western curve round from Springbank South, then an Up loop line coming off to run behind West signal box of 40 levers which was renewed on 5th. February 1923. To the south here was the New yard of 21 sidings, while opposite on the Down side, where the corresponding loop came in was the Top yard of six sidings. Further along, where Springhead West No. 2 (Springhead Sidings) was situated, the Up loop melted into the Storage and New sidings, more of New yard and the Jubilee sidings of 21 roads. The latter signal box was opened on 8th. June 1907 and lasted until 1944. There were four lengthy reception sidings for Down arrivals running parallel to the goods loop which were controlled by possibly the route indicating signal on the H & B worked by Locomotive Jc., where the main running lines were rejoined.

The Neptune Street branch

Before sallying forth westwards, however, a trip down the southern branch to Neptune Street would be profitable, beginning with Springbank South Jc., where the two arms of the triangle converged, with a signal box of twenty levers on the west side and the crossing of the Anlaby road by a bridge adjacent to another over Boothferry road which was the other widened in 1923 to three tracks to take here the branch off to Dairycoates goods sidings, 60 chains long and with a gradient of 1 in 120. The depot was opened on 1st. May 1905 as a relief to Neptune Street and had access to Hessle road close by the NER level crossing. In LNER days there was access by way of a siding to the NER Chalk Lane engineer's yard and on to the 'straight' line, though nothing of importance. On the main line which ran past the football ground, the BR opened a halt at Boothferry Park on 6th. January 1951 for home games, ¼ mile from Springbank South and eight minutes away from Paragon station. Running south the line crossed at an angle just north of Hessle Road crossing, in fact, the bowstring bridge passed within a whisker of the signal box there, reducing the site somewhat. From here the line ran parallel to the NE activity whch served the docks directly, the H & B on the landward side and with no connection between the two, apart from an odd siding. Later on in the history of the independent companies, however, in 1914 the NER built a double track junction at Liverpool Street, the signal box of twenty levers opening in May 1914 but soon closing in 1917. By this means it was possible for traffic off the NER to be moved to and from Springhead. This was in fact the second successful attempt at a link; much earlier there had been a proposal to run a spur from Burleigh Street to Wilmington, bridge abutments and earthworks were constructed, but nothing further transpired. Instead the formation became the long Stoneferry road branch, with sidings for the British Extracting Company (see p 46).

Neptune Street was the chief goods depot, built with its length along

Beverley Road station at the end of Fitzeroy street. Modern buildings on the same site look just as menacing today. *C. T. Goode*

Jackson street and end facing Neptune street. It had three gables and fifteen bays, served by five lines and equipped with electric cranes. The signal box here was a large one of 60 levers, managing the small yards for arrivals and departures, coal and emties sidings, plus the entrance to Billingsgate fish depot. There were probably more miniature ground signal arms in use here (19) than anywhere else on the system. The box closed on 31st. January 1938 and was known for a time as Subway Jc., along with another NER cabin close by, which caused confusion. The Dairycoates subway ran beneath the lines at this point to St. Andrew's dock from West Dock avenue.

Springhead to South Cave

With the yards and goods lines to the south of it, the main line had run along to Locomotive Jc. without impediment, apart from a slop across it at that signal box to transfer wagons into Springhead works and engine sheds on the north side. More will be forthcoming about this complex in the next chapter. Locomotive Jc. had 50 levers and was a very important location at the west end of all the goods and servicing activities. It is rather amusing to note that all the traffic in and out of the works and sheds had to be signalled out by means of one ground disc, No. 38! No ceremony here. After a dip down at 1 in 150, which was certainly handy to get a good run, the line began its climb to Little Weighton at 1 in 125, stiffening to 1 in 101 through Willerby & Kirkella-the bark of the 2-8-0s as they tackled this made the rafters ring around the district. For safety reasons there was an extra outer Home signal, No. 36 near the foot of the gradient for inbound coal trains, plus an illuminated track circuit. With the introduction of regular interval passenger services a new halt was provided at Springhead, of wooden construction and opened from 8th. April 1929. Actually it was north of Anlaby village and served a group of railwaymen's houses. Its location marked the original site of a station planned her, which never materialised in 1885.

At 1 mile 1185 yd. across playing fields and well wooded land the line reached Willerby & Kirkella station, with a fine building almost the twin of its pair at North Cave, both on the Down side with the stationmaster's house and booking office at ground level below the general waiting room and ladies' room, plus some private accommodation upstairs at platform level. The building was let into the embarkment with its platform, while that on the Up side had a neat and solid wooden waiting shed with a good awning complementary to that on the main building. From the booking office steps led up to the Hull platform, while a subway in glazed tiles led across to the other side, ending up in a covered walkway. The whole effect was pleasing and the station was popular with season ticket holders, being only 14 minutes from Hull. There was early bus competition which ran from Kirkella nearby. The stationmaster would point out in conversation that the building, up against the embankment and facing north, was always damp and that the family and staff were, even in LNER days, allowed but three paraffin lamps to light the whole house and public rooms!

The Up starting signal No. 13 by the signal box, here of levers was replaced at some stage by an NER type slotted signal with a sharpened end for a finial instead of the usual metalwork on top, not a very edifying spectacle, and it is significant that the item was left on site long after everything else had vanished.

From Willerby the H & B had a spectacular run up to Little Weighton, at 3 miles 698 yd. up at 1 in 100 or 110, a taxing climb for the small domeless 0-6-0s with the empties or indeed for anything attached to anything like a good load. It was soon decided to ease the signalling of trains on this section and to make room for the incapacitated by opening up an Up goods line from a signal box at Kirkella Cutting (20 levers), opened in 1896 and running for exactly half a mile to its exit at Eppleworth (16 levers), on the same side of the line as Kirkella Cutting. On the same side again at the latter place was a long siding with lines off into the company gravel pit and chalk quarry. During the last major war naval ammunition was stored here, while rumour had it in wartime of the presence of a large rail-mounted gun hereabouts which may have had a home here. All the loop and siding installation seems to have gone by 3rd.June 1956, leaving an intermediate colour light signal on the Up line just before Eppleworth viaduct, a feature locally, of five arches. A station was planned here and the gradient was eased for this purpose. The idea lapsed and opportunity was taken to put in the aforementioned Up loop, which was open for use on 1st. June 1908.

Between two more cuttings was sited the small section splitter of Skidby, of seven levers on the Down side whose signalman had no points to work, only to admire the flora and fauna and pull off signals as required. The post disappeared during 1917. The second of the two cuttings was a winner, of 83 ft. at its deepest and with almost sheer white chalky sides. Originally the workings were called Big Hill, later Little Weighton cutting, from which some 900,000 cubic yards of chalk were removed to create the embankments in the Hull area. This was taken by the unusual method of tunnelling the railway temporarily and sinking shafts to it, down which the spoil was dropped, to be taken away in wagonloads.

Once out of the cutting Little Weigton station was reached, guarded by a very tall Home signal, No. 15 situated on the right hand side for better viewing by drivers. The equivalent Homes, No. 9 for eastbound trains were equally tall and were a pair of repeaters one above the other, due to an intervening bridge. The station building was on the Down side and was of the B pattern, as found at Drax and Carlton, in which the two storey stationmaster's house was attached to a single storey block of waiting rooms, having a gable at the end of the run. At the time of writing, all three of the above survive; Carton still has a line passing through the site running to the power station at Drax. Here again were the excellent platform awnings supported on four pillars. At Little Weighton the waiting shed on the Up side was originally similar to that at Willerby, but had been replaced by an inferior looking NER construction with a tilted roof. The goods yard was on the Up side, as was a chalk pit served by an extension of one of the yard sidings. There was also a long refuge siding on the Down side, the tail of whch ran into another chalk pit. There was little about the village here to commend it, and not much revenue; one would imagine the station at the mouth of Drewton tunnel was one of the little signal boxes, Drewton East of 11 levers, opened in 1914 to divide the block section and which had provision to operate a facing point into the long Down refuge siding, so turning this into a loop if it were needed. Nothing was heard of the suggestion after 1914. The cabin was destroyed by fire in May 1929.

From this point the line ran steadily downhill at 1 in 150 for about seven miles, not quite as stiff as on the Hull side of the hump. The tunnel, originally to be called Riplingham, was 2,116 yd. long and the longest on the H & B. At first its length was to be only 1,710 yd. with four ventilating shafts. This was revised, however, as the tunnel was extended from the western end, giving a final total of five shafts, the tops of which were a

Springbank North signal box with the large H & B bracket signal and NE style replacement on the left. *C. T. Goode*

distinctive feature of the landscape. In certain atmospheric conditions these used to emit steam, a condition which still prevails on occasion, some thirty years after closure. There was much activity around the construction sites, with materials for buildings and bridges brought by road from Hessle in a continuous flow. Some 8,000 navvies were employed, aged from ten to seventy, large numbers being Scots or Irish who spent quite a lot of time fighting each other. The largest camp was at Riplingham, close to the tunnel workings with its own shops and church, while some men lived in huts alongside the course of the line, many with their families. In Hull, camps were at Hull bridge, Wyke street and Springhead. Children at the Riplingham camp went to school in Little Weighton. In 1882, because of rioting between the Celtic factions a total of 200 of each nationally were fired; the unrest was probably due to payments since the men worked from dawn to dusk, about 58 hours for £1.50 per week. There was a strike in May 1881 for an extra 2½d a week, and in July 1884 all work was halted for five months as the company was in financial difficulties. The men were laid off but remained on the site. When completed after five years of work, the tunnel was a straight one, apart from a slight curve at the east end, between 18 and 19 ft. in height, of 25 ft. span with brick portals and lined in brick throughout. The five shafts were each 11 ft. 6 in. in diameter.

Outside the west end of the tunnel, on the Up side was the small five lever Drewton West cabin, which came and went just as mysteriously, probably in 1917. Even its location is uncertain, some placing it on the Down side, from which it controlled only that direction of running, a somewhat boring occupation, one would imagine. The two small tunnels of Sugar Loaf and Weedley of 132 yd. each were real enough, as was Weedley signal box between them which had five levers and enjoyed a most idyllic location with the rolling hills and a spring of clear water nearby. The box closed on 5th. September 1932, leaving its brick base to last as long as did the line. The Down home signal here was another very tall one, providing much exercise for the lampman, on the wrong side the line. One speculates as to how signalmen reached this location, other than by levitation or living on the job. Roads were, and still are, in short supply in this area. Probably because the difficulty was realised, the scrapping of the block post caused a Down semi-automatic colour light Home signal with its attendant distant to appear in due course.

Still falling, the line entered South Cave station beneath the road bridge, under which was the ground frame for the Sand siding which led across the Down line into the small quarry. This was originally the property of John Kilner & Sons of Wakefield, for which they paid £644 in 1904. However, it did not last long, and on 18th. December 1908 there appeared another application for its reinstatement by Mr. T.H. Lyon. This was carried out at a cost of £240 to house four wagons in January 1909. In later years the pit was owned by Yorkshire Amalgamated Products (YAP).

South Cave station lay to the north of the village, about twenty minutes walk away from it, and the amount of traffic generated was not unusually heavy, certainly not to justify the size of the premises which were one of the two largest on the system, the other being Howden. The main buildings were on the south side and were of twin gables, half timbered fashion. The station master lived here and the building was linked by the booking office, parcels and general waiting room to the end gabled section which housed the ladies' rooms. Kitchens and a refreshment room were planned for this end of the building but were never completed. At Howden the Class A plan was identical but reversed, with the road elevation facing the platforms. Once reason for the extraordinary size of South Cave station, which looked well from the north side at a distance, was the proximity of the Hotham estate. The Down side had a rather squashed form of waiting shed which was unique to this particular location. Its awning, too, was not level with that on the main building. Water supplies were available here for trains in each direction, and a supply tank was placed at the east end beyond the road bridge. After about 1906, however, Carlton, further west, became the preferred station for replenishment. The maintenance men for the signalling on the line had a depot at South Cave, while Howden was home to two sets of company painters and decorators.

Once through North Cave station the line levelled off at Stoney Lane crossing, the first crossing on the line, an indication of the flat terrain to come.

Springhead Works

The Hull & Barnsley opened shop with 42 locomotives designed by its first consultant engineer W. Kirtley of the London, Chatham & Dover Railway, all of which were based at the Hull end and housed in a shed at the north side of the line with water tank, cranes and coaling stages of wood. The site was near Springhead waterworks on land which was bought from Trinity House, who had a farm nearby. As mentioned, the south side of the line was given over to various sets of sidings, and the whole complex became known as Springhead. The first resident Chief Mechanical Engineer was Matthew Stirling, son of Patrick of GNR fame, a man who had served his time at Doncaster works and had had duties at Doncaster and Peterborough. On his arrival he bought with him useful colleagues to the footplate from both the GN and NE companies, so that there was no shortage of men to move the machines. Stirling regarded his first problem as the hardness of the local water supply, which was soon attended to, then a supply of wagons, 550 high sided and 150 low sided four wheelers. New acquisitions were to come from contractors, but repairs could be done by the company itself, a useful dogma in view of the fact that the company had been pressed to find extra money since 1884.

However, Stirling continued to apply to his board of management and was successful in building up piece by piece at Springhead; first a stores in January 1886, then a workshop a year later which formed an early part of the loco. works. Materials were moved to the site from the NER 'straight' line at Waterworks crossing, from where a long single line branch went alongside the construction site to the waterworks down at the end of Springbank west. This line was later linked to the railway works through a point into a siding.

Gradually the stock of locomotives was increasing and two new overhead travelling cranes were installed to enable repairs to proceed. The original wagon shop could cope with only three vehicles at a time, so in 1892 a proper wagon works was asked for, which was eventually authorised, along with a much welcomed extension to the engine shed, a boiler and engine house. The wagon works were 335 x 90 ft. and could manage 100 wagons at a time.

By 1906 the engine shed, though expanded, could only cover 72 locomotives out of a fleet of 116, so that it was duly extended by 200 ft. at the east end. A new coaling stage in the style of the GN one at New England, and a 55 ft. turntable were put in.

There were now 3,800 wagons, so an additional wagon shop appeared in 1909, as well as a new carriage shop of 170 x 60 ft. to deal with all

Springhead Works from Locomotive Jc. signal box on a winters' day in 1962. The Little Weighton pick-up is approaching. *M . Haddon*

The layout at Botanic crossing, looking south. Lines to Anlaby Road right being taken by WD No. 90677. Centre to Paragon and left to shed. 21.3.67. M Nicholson

coach servicing. The small carriage shop on the north side of the new erecting shop now became the loco. paint shop. The site of the works was now almost totally completed by the addition of a pattern shop, smithy and machine shop. A petrol vacuum cleaner appeared to keep the coaching stock spick and span. With a locomotive stock of 118, the works staff on that side of the business numbered 330, while carriage and wagon depts were 238, overseeing 138 coaches and 4,827 wagons, making an awful lot of buffers. The sidings were indeed full.

On takeover by the NER in 1922 all the best machinery and men, 230 in all, went to Darlington, though heavy loco. repairs were still carried out at Springhead and some were sent round from Dairycoates. The carriage works closed in 1922, becoming part of the wagon works which kept afloat until 1971, doing well with up to 400 wagons repaired weekly in 1964. The engine shed had 122 occupants in 1923, falling to 70 in 1929 and 28 by 1950, finally closing on 1st. December 1958.

Stepney, looking east with signal box and crossing. *C. T. Goode*

The Victoria Dock branch

The Victoria Dock branch curved away from West Parade signal box outside Paragon to the north, accompanied by two lines leading to Botanic Gardens shed, a smallish place on the east side. The lines ran parallel with the Anlaby loop for a short way, to join together at Botanic Gardens crossing, first taking in a northern exit from the shed. The corner of Princes avenue and Springbank was a busy one, with plenty of trams and their wiring to take into account at the crossing. To the west were the gardens, later Hymers College and the ceremonial gates to the cemetery which were removed, to be replaced in due course by a row of shops. Almost everyone knows, perhaps, that the station across the road, a very cramped affair, was known as Cemetery Gates at first, finally becoming Botanic Gardens. The station was popular for trips to the coast and there was a coal yard here on the avenue side. The Up home signal was extremely tall and made a great spectacle for the back windows of the houses in Louis street nearby. The line continued to turn until it ran eastwards over Park Road level crossing with its little wooden cabin to Stepney station situated just west of Beverley road, a pleasing building of two storeys with two gables, facing south. Not much in the mileage lay between the station, with Botanic Gardens at 1 mile from Paragon and Stepney at 2¾ miles, much less if one walked up Beverley road. Opposite Stepney station across the level crossing was Temple street goods yard on the north side of the line, with a facing connection beyond the level crossing where yet more trams were to be found. The signal box was built very close to the public house next to it; some considered that the signalman had private access through the side of the box! Part of the goods yard ran into the other yard on the east side of the bowstring bridge which led the H & B line into Cannon Street, called Stepney goods yard, a bigger affair with a large goods shed and coal depot with access to the river Hull. A signal box at the end of the layout, at Wincolmlee which also worked a level crossing at Bankside, dealt with traffic, including a further small yard on the south side. Wincolmlee had some 30 levers, most of which went spare when the yards were closed. The site was half a mile from Stepney and a mere fifty yards from Wilmington swing bridge, giving the observers on the ground the impression that the signalling here was NER lavishness par excellence; in actual fact the bridge was not a block post and the

Wilmington Station. *C. T. Goode*

presence of trains was only indicated there for operating purposes. The next post was Wilmington Station, 530 yd. away. The bridge carried a very useful public footpath on its north side which has served to keep it in business, albeit in a modest way up to the time of writing.

Wilmington station, essentially for work people at the vast industrial site here, with a mixture of oil and cake mills, flour, fuel oil, tar, varnish and confectionery all rubbing shoulders with each other, served nevertheless several closely packed streets of houses with their own picture theatre and competing tram service, on Cleveland street which with their own picture theatre and competing tram service, managed to pass beneath the line by a gloomy bridge carrying five tracks at its junction with the Hornsea branch. The junction was a fairly elaborate affair just off the end of the island platform constructed in the style of the final version of Brough, with wooden platform buildings but with the brick booking office and staff facilities at the tunnel entry off Foster street on the north side. Round the corner on the Hornsea branch at 733 yd. was Wilmington East signal box just beyond where the H & B line crossed above it, controlling a small yard on the north side of the line.

As the line began to curve away to the south east, a view was offered of the H & B line close by, running parallel at a higher level and crossing the Hornsea branch and the Foredyke stream in quick succession, both crossings made by largish girder bridges linked by a brick viaduct of four arches over a marshy stretch of land. The assembly was completed by a further arch and a girder bridge over Dansom lane. The NER line brought round with it from Wilmington a couple of goods lines, off which went sidings to Wilmington goods depot and coal depot, both of which fronted on to Cleveland street. One goods line now accompanied the running lines across the Foredyke stream to run to another small coal depot, and the lines reverted to Up and Down only at Dansom Lane level crossing, 688 yd. trom Wilmington, where were the Phoenix Soap works, a Mission room and Saw mill.

Just before Southcoates station (537 yd.) the line crossed Holderness road, the main way out to the coast, on the level, and passed each side of the island platform here which was again in the style of Wilmington and Brough, this time with all facilities contained in the platform offices. From the skew footbridge looking south was the vista of a vast timber yard and 28 or so sidings which made their way over Hedon road into Victoria Dock. There was a goods depot and also a shed and coal depot. This supplemented a larger one which ran along the northern flank of the station area. The view from the level crossing southwards was framed by one of those impressive signal gantries carrying lots of small arms. Southcoates was a very popular station with the football ground next to it in Craven street and with a population anxious to escape from time to time from the teeming warren of terraces containing houses with no roadways attached but with little walks and tiny gardens separating each row. Names reflected the sociable and jovial; Minnie's, Cissie's, Harold's,

Walter's or Herbert's terrace, all within shouting distance of the railway and some too close to industry for comfort and health.

The line to Hedon

Round sharply eastwards now, and beneath Craven street bridge and the H & B line to Alexandra dock, picking up more dock lines again but making no physical connection. Somewhere round here was a siding called Sweet Dews, to which various wagons would be sent from far flung points on the system. The author has not so far pinpointed its whereabouts but knows that Sweet Dews farm existed to the north on Newbridge road.

Marfleet station, 1 mile 1,347 yd. was a poor thing of simple buildings and platforms and a couple of sidings off on the Up side. The signal box had a generous 25 levers, of which half were spare; the catchment area was originally very sparse and it was only in the latter days of the station, which closed earlier than the rest on the branch, that the large Greatfield housing estate sprang up to the north, too late to be of much use as a revenue earner. Marfleet village lay to the south, just north of Hedon road.

The course of the line now lay through featureless country, more or less straight on for 3 miles 192 yd. to Hedon station, relieved only by the interesting site of the race course which lay east of the Preston-Saltend road and ran along the south side of the line virtually to the small township. Racing in Hull began, perhaps surprisingly, with a course on Anlaby road years before that at Hedon, where some 287 acres were purchased for use at a cost of £75,000. The stewards here included many of the most influential and wealthy of the district, such as Lord Zetland and the Earl of Yarborough, and the first meeting was a two day event on 24th. May 1888. The railway, when approached, seemed to be keen on the idea and offered a special service of 24 extra trains leaving Paragon at five minute intervals; however, these did not materialise, in fact, over the years even fewer trains ran. This happened even when a halt was provided at the course, though it was probably at a disadvantage as the grandstand lay at the Hedon road side of the course. During the next seven years eleven meetings were held, not a very encouraging prospect which led to the dissolving of the company involved in the venture in 1895. There was a revival in 1901 when the Hull Racecourse Company was formed, running four meetings before they, too, were wound up on 11th. September 1909, at which time the halt presumably became redundant too. The next rumour of a revival came in 1922, but nothing came of it and the grandstand was sold in 1924. After this the land became an airfield which was opened by Prince George on 10th. September 1929 and managed under the aegus of the Hull Corporation Airfield Company until final closure in 1951. Various concerns began flying commercially from here as developments went ahead, chiefly the KLM Dutch Airways which commenced operations between Amsterdam and Liverpool, calling at Hedon from 31st. May 1934. Flights left Hull at 11.30 a.m., reaching Hull at 18.50 and going forward to Liverpool at 19.05. Provincial Airways flew to Grimsby at 8.15 a.m., while Hillman's Airways took off for Belfast at 9.30 a.m. Aberdeen Airways called in both directions, at 17.15 for Aberdeen and 18.15 for London. A promising start and an interesting slice of local history which is most pleasant to record, even though it is not strictly railway. Hull Corporation desired greater support from the general public, which was not forthcoming, with the result that KLM threatened to end its services, giving the frosty reason that Northerners were not air-minded, also, that accidents had unfortunately depleted the stock of available aircraft. These threats came in July 1935, and after a further month or two the company switched to Doncaster, where they continued to operate until war came.

The aerodrome was certainly used during hostilities. In January 1947 the 'Sporting Life' announced that the aerodrome was to become a race course again; in the event the actuality became a speedway track which appeared in 1948 and, wonder of wonders, the halt was reopened for a short period between August and November of that year, after which nothing further was heard of it.

A Hedon the station was just at the north end of the town at a level crossing with the road to Preston. As originally laid, the line was single through the station with a platform on the south side only and a sort of passing loop available with the small signal box next to the station building. Things were altered in 1903 after the line was doubled as far as here from Hull, leaving a messy track layout, by which passenger trains both ways had to use the single platform, as the 'sort of passing loop', though still in position, was not available as such. An enlarged signal box of thirty levers was resited on the opposite side of the line by the level crossing.

Passenger services

Over the past century and a half of railway refinement and development there have been so many changes that it would be folly to try to illustrate all of them, or to select the years in which each took place; suffice it, therefore, to choose several periods in the history of railway services in the area, in the hope that it will give an idea of what was on offer to the public. In this it is hoped that nothing momentous has been left out.

There were of course four tracks out along the Humber bank to Staddle thorpe Jc. (Gilberdyke), all well used as will be seen. Over the years

A B1 hurries the afternoon fish through Hessle, with admirers. *C. T. Goode*

they won the 'Prize Length' award for upkeep and appearance, as well as a place in the records for the longest straight stretch in the country. The prime service was that to and from King's Cross, taking much longer than today's 2½ hours, with the only through train of the day before 1914 taking eight minutes under four hours, leaving at 9.43 a.m., with its opposite number leaving King's Cross at 6.05 p.m. and reaching Hull direct at 10.12 p.m. Other services to London left at 11.30 a.m. and 5.05p.m. as through carriages transferred at Doncaster, with connecting services off the 7.18 a.m., 3.20 and 11.25 p.m. Through carriages arrived at Hull with the 2.29 and 4.59 p.m., while there were connections at Doncaster into the 8.12 and 11.57 a.m., 3.35, 5.35, 6.13 and 8.32 p.m., also the 1.32 a.m. arrivals, also at Selby into the 9.52 a.m., 2.02 and 4.42 p.m. arrivals, giving a choice of routes for the passenger, who did not however have any option but to go via Selby on Sundays, due to the whim of the landowner at Saltmarshe who forbade such mechanical romps over his land on the Sabbath.

Sundays 1914

Hull	dep:	11.40a.m.	4.27p.m.	8.05
		*		
King's Cross	arr:	4.40p.m.	9.23	3.10a.m.

King's Cross	dep:	11.40a.m.	5.00p.m.	8.45
Hull	arr:	4.59p.m.	11.25	4.42a.m.

* through carriage All via Selby

The Doncaster branch via Goole does not appear to have been unduly overworked by passenger trains up to 1914, even with its importance as a carrier for London traffic and with its potential for Midlands and south-west traffic. Sheffield services seem to have been included as part of the Great Central runs beyond to Manchester and Liverpool. These left Hull at 6.20 and 10.52 a.m., taking four hours to Liverpool Cen, at 2.55 p.m. to Manchester taking three hours, and finally at 6.12 p.m., reaching Liverpool in a little over the four hours. There were also five other services each way between Hull and Sheffield, involving a change at Doncaster, with the total run taking 2-2½ hours. Arrivals from Liverpool by through service reached Hull via Doncaster at 2.29, 5.35 and 8.32 p.m., the 5.35 managing things very well in 3¾ hours. With the veto in force on Sundays, the trains via Selby were as follows:

1914

Hull	dep:	11.40p.m.	4.27
Doncaster	arr:	1.11p.m.	6.05
Sheffield	arr:	3.47	6.05

Ex GC B2 4-6-0 and NE B16 4-6-0 making a race of it near Hessle.
Coll: C. T. Goode

Sheffield	dep:	2.00a.m.	"
Doncaster	arr:	3.07	8.50p.m. (dep)
Hull	arr:	4.59	11.25p.m.

The reader is now in the realms of 'foreign' engines, namely those of the GCR which brought in the expresses and which would stay overnight on shed before working out on an early run the following day. These were handsome green creations, of a darker hue than the NER and certainly more arresting than the sombre black of the L & Y 'foreigners' which came into Hull via Goole from the Liverpool Exchange, using the relatively easily graded L & Y route via Goole and along the Calder valley; this was reflected in the running time of 3 hours 15 minutes by the 9.05 a.m. from Hull, with the evening 6.40 p.m. taking somewhat longer. From Liverpool the expresses reached Hull at 12.43 p.m. (non-stop from Goole) and 5.13 p.m., the latter taking the palm with a run of 3 hours 3 minutes and the nice touch of a booked stop at Hessle only, between Goole and Hull!

There were also trains to Halifax, worked by the NER at 8.55, 11.00 a.m. and 3.20 p.m., with two arrivals in Hull at 10.57 a.m. and 4.10 p.m. The running time for these trains was about 2¼ hours and the route was through Selby and Normanton and on to the L & Y through Wakefield and Low Moor.

The third 'foreigner' to enter Hull with express services was the LNWR with its interesting locomotive in 'blackberry' black, so called because of its similarity to the lustre on the fruit, lined in red and white, all very smart and usually with heroic or intellectual nameplates. 'John Keats' was one of the 'Prince of Wales' 4-6-0s which came regularly to Hull with the Liverpool expresses. There were three arrivals via Leeds and Selby, at 2.34, 735 p.m. and a late 12.43 a.m., the latter with the footnote: 'calls at any station to set down only'. Out of Hull went the 9.20 a.m., 2.05 and 4.00 p.m., the fastest run of the day being made by the first, in 3 hours 20 minutes, which also managed to call at Brough if necessary on Tues. and Thurs. to take up for Leeds and beyond. For some reason the inbound 2.34 p.m. arrival stopped at Staddlethorpe Jc. only, between Selby and Hull; the ways of the operating department were indeed strange!

To summarise the main express departures for Liverpool from Hull:

6.20 a.m. GC to Central. 9.05 a.m. L & Y to Exchange.

9.20 a.m. LNW to Lime Street. 10.52 a.m. GC to Central.

2.05 p.m. LNW to Lime Street. 4.00 p.m. LNW to Lime Street.

6.12 p.m. GC to Central. 6.40 p.m. L & Y to Exchange.

Next follows a table of trains along the Hull-Leeds line, excluding the express workings mentioned above, but with the Halifax services and two trains in each direction for Sheffield via Church Fenton, one of which divided, shedding a Halifax portion at Selby. Apart from the places served enroute, there was little gained by this service over that through Doncaster, as the timing, of about two hours, was the same. It recalled a former attempt by the Midland Railway to operate between Sheffield and Hull between 1883 and 1888, running via Normanton, Milford Jc. and Selby, and bringing yet another foreign locomotive into the town in a distinctive crimson colour. The duration of journeys indicates at how many stations the trains would stop, with some taking two hours to reach Leeds.

Hull to Leeds line. 1914. (weekdays)

Dep 6.05a.m.	arr. Burton Salmon	8.02a.m.	Slow
7.18	arr. Leeds	9.15	Slow
8.25	arr. Leeds	9.34	Non-stop
8.55	arr. Halifax	11.10	
9.36	arr. Sheffield	11.23	via Selby
10.15	arr. Leeds	12.09p.m.	
11.00	arr. Halifax	1.11	
12.30p.m.	arr. Leeds	2.23	Slow
2.44	arr. Leeds	4.39	Slow
3.20	arr. Sheffield	5.19	fast to Selby
	arr. Halifax	5.25	divides
3.55	arr. Selby	5.00	Tues. only. Slow

Class D 20 No. 62396 on the 4.27 p.m. to Bridlington. *J. Frank*

Dep 5.14p.m.	arr. Leeds	6.51	
5.55	arr. Leeds	7.52	
8.05	arr. Selby	9.08p.m.	Slow
8.40	arr. Normanton	9.57a.m.	Express
	arr. Leeds	10.13	divides at Selby
11.23	arr. Selby	12.18a.m.	Slow

Sundays

Dep 6.50a.m.	arr. Leeds	9.12	Slow
11.40	arr. Selby	12.30p.m.	
4.27p.m.	arr. Selby	5.22	
8.05	arr. Normanton	9.57	

The pattern of movement was now more or less settled up to the outbreak of war in 1939, and during this conflict the major services survived quite well, all considered, with one through service from Hull to King's Cross at 9. a.m., arrive at 2.20 p.m. and a return from the capital at 1.25 p.m., back in Hull at 6.31 p.m. There were two departures for Liverpool Cen. via Sheffield, at 9.20 a.m. and 4.05 p.m., each taking about five hours with most of the important stops en route. The 9.20 a.m. also ran on Sundays and took one hour longer. Arrivals in Hull were at 2.26 p.m. and 9.28 p.m., the latter also on Sundays. The author well remembers these trains during wartime, living next to the old GC line and noting the D 49 motive power, always in good external condition, thanks to the female cleaners at Botanic, no doubt.

The old LNW route through Leeds and Huddersfield saw arrivals from Liverpool Lime St. into Hull at 3.00 p.m. and 7.55 p.m., both taking a round four hours, with departures from Hull at 2.00 and 3.55 p.m. The 2.00 was booked for the run to be completed in 3¼ hours, remarkable for the period. For the Goole and Wakefield customers there was nothing through to Liverpool Exchange, only an express to Wakefield at 6.35 p.m. by which Liverpool could be reached in due course at 10.38 p.m. The train's arrival in Hull was 1.00 p.m., for which Liverpool had been left at 9.09 a.m.

It looks, therefore, as if during wartime much effort was put into keeping the LNER trans-pennine service in business at the expense of the others, though the Leeds route won hands down for speed.

Trains to Doncaster numbered seven on weekdays, five on Sundays, and all either ran to Sheffield Victoria or had a connection. The reverse number was the same. Probably for war workers, a train left Hull for Stainforth at 8.05 a.m., balanced by a service from Throne North at 5.12 p.m. shown as one class only, probably a railcar. Both of these latter were all-stations. Other trains to Leeds at the same time as above were about ten in number, with five on Sundays. The slowest run, stopping everywhere,

B1 No. 61171 leaves Beverley on a York-Hull service. 10/9/55
The Midland Railway Trust Ltd.

including Broomfleet and Marsh Lane, was the 5.30 p.m. which took 4 minutes short of two hours. Perhaps the most interesting train was one which ran every day of the week, probably with the mail, leaving Hull at 8.40 p.m., then running express to Selby, where it divided, a portion going forward to Pontefract, arrival at 9.46 p.m. and Leeds at 10.12 p.m.

York could be reached off six trains by changing at Selby, with a journey time of about 1½ to 2 hours. Inbound to Hull, the service from Leeds was roughly similar, with one evening train leaving Sheffield Victoria at 7.05 p.m., running by way of Doncaster and Selby (dep. 10.35 p.m.) to reach Hull at 11.21 p.m., calling at Ferriby and Hessle to set down only. On Sundays, a morning train left Normanton at 8.07 a.m., then went all-stations Selby to Hull, arr. 10.11 a.m. This train, by the way, did a quickish turn round, leaving Hull at 11.25 a.m., Selby at 12.15 p.m. and back in Normanton at 12.42 p.m., probably a nice little job for the shed there.

York is mentioned above as a destination with a change at Selby; there was, of course the direct line through Beverley and Market Weighton, a good line, though one which never seemed to be used to its full capacity, probably because the other option passed through more lucrative stations. Pre 1914 there were eight trains each way on weekdays only, this due to the religious beliefs of the Hotham family, over whose land the line ran.

The slowest took 1 hour 35 min; there were, however, fast trains, the 5.05 p.m. from Hull which stopped at Beverley to take up only, then Market Weighton and Pocklington, arriving in York at 6.06 p.m. The morning 9.57 a.m. from york did the same in reverse, arriving in Hull at 11.00 a.m., while the 7.00 p.m. was booked to stop at Beverley and landed at 8.05 p.m.

The 1942 service showed seven trains each way on weekdays, with the 12.20 p.m. and 5.00 p.m. from Hull a buffet car; the inbound fast services had reached Hull at 11.28 a.m. and 4.09 p.m. respectively. Kiplingcotes, with the other wayside stations, managed three trains calling each way on weekdays.

Trains to Bridlington before 1914 were very generous, 14 each way on weekdays, eight of them, all stoppers, going through to Scarborough as did the 5.50 a.m. which not only demanded an unholy hour of getting up from its passengers, but staggered in at 8.14; or the 6.45 p.m. which arrived at 9.00 p.m., no doubt with ancient non-corridor coaches. The smart mover of the day was the 4.50 p.m. which ran non stop to Filey to reach there at 5.48 and Scarborough at 6.05 p.m. At 5.30 p.m. SX an express left Hull for Bridlington, to arrive at 6.10 p.m. And what of the morning trains for Hull? Best was the 8.22 a.m. from Scarborough which lingered a little as far as Bridlington, then took to its heels and ran non stop and arrived at 8.55. Such runs were excellent and have certainly never been repeated since. The overall roof at Beverley would have echoed finely as the fast trains rushed through. On Sundays there was one train each way stopping at every station:

Hull	dep:	7.00p.m.	Scarborough	dep:	5.00p.m.
Scarborough	arr:	9.20	Hull	arr:	7.28

Incidentally, to enjoy a day out by these trains, a passenger from Leeds would have had to set out at 2.54 a.m. and would not arrive back until 10.13 p.m.; such was advertised, but would perhaps only appeal to the dire railway enthusiast!

By 1942 the train service had dropped to eleven trains each way, but with two on Sundays. The first slow was now the 5.38, fast to Driffield, then Bridlington, followed however by the 5.50 doing all the stops to Scarborough. There was an express for Scarborough at 9.05 a.m. and one on Saturdays at 12.50 p.m., with the 4.50 p.m. SX express also. Beverley was now a booked stop for all trains except the 5.38 a.m. Being wartime, a slow left for Driffield at 9.30 p.m., arrive 10.10, turning round to leave at 10.28 p.m. with an arrival at 11.05 p.m., probably run with the visitors to Driffiled aerodrome in mind. There was nothing outstanding to Hull, except the 8.00 a.m. fast from Bridlington, arrive at 8.45 and the 8.16 a.m. out of Scarborough, arrive Hull at 9.38 a.m. The 7.00 a.m. was still running on Sundays, this time missing out Cayton and arriving in Scarborough at 9.14. There was also an evening train from Hull at 6.00 p.m. which ran fast to Beverley and Driffield, then Bridlington and slow

No. **189.** **Hull and Hornsea Bridge—Stock Special "Q."**
No. **188.** **Hull, Botanic Gardens and Hornsea—School Special.**
No. **182.** **Hull and Withernsea—School Special.**
Nos. **183** & **184.** **Hull, Wilmington and Withernsea—School Specials.**
Nos. **185.** & **190.** **Hull, Stepney and Withernsea—School Special.**

		188	190	182	189	183	185	184
					Q			
		a.m.	a.m.	a.m.	a.m.	a.m.	a.m.	a.m.
Hull ...	...dep.	8.15	8 20	8 28	9 10	9 20	9 25	9 30
Botanic Gardens	...arr.	8 19	—	—	—	—	—	9 34
,, ,,	...dep.	8 24	—	—	—	—	—	9 38
Stepney ...	...arr.	—	8 25	—	—	—	9 31	—
,, ...	...dep.	—	8 30	—	—	—	9 35	—
Wilmington	...arr.	8p29	8p33	8p38	9p18	9p28	9p38	9 43
,,	...dep.	—	—	—	—	—	—	9 47
Sutton-on-Hull	...arr.	—	—	—	9 25	—	—	—
,,	...dep.	—	—	—	9 35	—	—	—
Skirlaugh ...	...arr.	—	—	—	9 41	—	—	—
,, ...	...dep.	—	—	—	9 51	—	—	—
Ellerby ...	...pass	8 39	—	—	—	—	—	—
Hornsea Bridge	...arr. (c)	8 48	—	—	10 4	—	—	—
,, ,,	...dep.	8 53	—	—	—	—	—	—
Hornsea	...arr.	8 55	—	—	—	—	—	—
Southcoates	...pass	—	—	—	—	9 33	—	9 52
Hedon ...	✠ ,,	—	8 45	8 52	—	9 43	9 50	10 2
Rye Hill ...	✠ ,,	—	8 50	8 57	—	9 48	9 55	10 7
Ottringham	✠ ,,	—	8 59	9 6	—	9 54	10 3	10 14
Winestead	✠ ,,	—	9 4	9 14	—	9 59	10 9	10 19
Patrington	...arr. (c)	—	9 5	9 15	—	10 0	10 10	10 20
,,	...dep.	—	9 10	9 20	—	10 5	10 15	10 25
Withernsea	...arr.	—	9 17	9 28	—	10 12	10 22	10 32

		188	183	184	182	189	185	190
						Q		
		p.m.	p.m.	p.m.	p.m.	p.m.	p.m.	p.m.
Withernsea	...dep.	—	7 5	7 12	7 25	—	8 20	8 30
Winestead	✠pass	—	7 12	7 20	7 33	—	8 28	8 38
Ottringham	✠ ,,	—	7 18	7 26	7 39	—	8 33	8 43
Rye Hill ...	✠ ,,	—	7 24	7 33	7 47	—	8 40	8 50
Hedon ...	✠ ,,	—	7 29	7 38	7 53	—	8 45	8 55
Southcoates	... ,,	—	7 39	7 47	—	—	—	—
Hornsea	...dep.	7 0	—	—	—	—	—	—
Hornsea Bridge	... ,,	—	—	—	—	7 40	—	—
Ellerby ...	...pass	7 12	—	—	—	—	—	—
Skirlaugh ...	...arr.	—	—	—	—	7 54	—	—
,, ...	...dep.	—	—	—	—	8 2	—	—
Sutton-on-Hull	...arr.	—	—	—	—	8 8	—	—
,,	...dep.	—	—	—	—	8 16	—	—
Wilmington	...arr.	7p22	7 44	7 52	8p10	8p22	8p55	9 p 7
,,	...dep.	—	7 47	7 55	—	—	—	—
Stepney ...	...arr.	—	7 51	7 59	—	—	8 58	9 10
,, ...	...dep.	—	7 54	8 2	—	—	9 1	9 14
Botanic Gardens	...arr.	7 27	—	8 5	—	—	—	—
,, ,,	...dep.	7 31	—	8 8	—	—	—	—
Hull ...	...arr.	7 35	8 0	8 12	8 20	8 30	9 6	9 20

THURSDAY, 16th JULY—continued. 1925

No. **182.**—Stock—13 T, 2 B.

Conveys St. Stephen's S.S. (100 adults, 180 juveniles) and Thornton Xall S.S. (100 adults, 400 juveniles).

No. **183.**—Stock—19 T, 2 B.

Conveys King's Hall S.S. (1st Party), (200 adults, 600 juveniles), St. George's Road Wes. S.S. (100 adults, 300 juveniles) ex Hull.

No. **184.**—Stock—18 T, 2 B.

Conveys Gospel Hall S.S. (55 adults, 150 juveniles) and King's Hall S.S. (100 adults, 200 juveniles) ex Hull ; Newland Wes. S.S. (75 adults, 200 juveniles) ex Botanic Gardens ; King's Hall S.S. (100 adults, 200 juveniles) ex Wilmington.

No. **185.**—Stock—11 T, 2 B.

Conveys Salvation Army Icehouse S.S. (160 adults, 320 juveniles) ex Hull ; People's Mission (50 adults, 80 juveniles) ex Stepney.

No. **188.**—Stock—13 T, 2 B.

Conveys Albion Cong. S.S. (24 adults, 120 juveniles), Parkin's S.S. party, Park Street Unitarian S.S. (35 adults, 80 children) ex Hull ; Lambert Street P.M. (150 adults, 250 children) ex Botanic Gardens.

No. **189.**—Stock—1 B.

Copy of Guards' Journal to be sent to this Office.

No. **190.**—Stock—10 T, 2 B.

Conveys Hessle Road Cong. S.S. party (60 adults, 150 juveniles) ex Hull ; Newland Wes. S.S. party (80 adults, 250 juveniles) ex Stepney.

Ordinary trains to be strengthened as under in addition to usual Thursday's strengthening :—

Train.	From	To	WT	Return Working, etc.
9 46 a.m.	Hull	Hornsea ...	1	10-45 a.m.
11 58 a.m.	,, ...	,, ...	2	12-59 p.m.
1 20 p.m.	,, ...	,, ...	3	As required.
2 8 p.m.	,, ...	,, ...	2	3-8 p.m.
5 42 p.m.	,, ...	,, ...	2	6-35 p.m.
6 33 p.m.	,, ...	,, ...	2	7-30 p.m.
9 0 p.m.	,, ...	,, ...	3	10-0 p.m.

Hornsea Bridge Box to be open from 7-0 a.m. until Stock Specials have left.

Hull and Hornsea Goods Train to leave 6-0 a.m. and run correspondingly earlier.

No. **181.** **Hull to Wembley Hill—Guaranteed Excursion.**

E.P.

		a.m.			p.m.
Hull	...dep.	7 0	Doncaster... ...	...arr.	11 48
Staddlethorpe ...	...pass	7 25	,, ...	...dep.	11 52
Goole	... ,,	7 36	Thorne Jct. ...	...pass	12 5
Thorne Jct. ...	... ,,	7 50	Goole	... ,,	12 19
Doncaster... ...	...arr.	8 4	Staddlethorpe ...	... ,,	12 29
			Hull	...arr.	12 53

Stock—2 Restaurant Cars, 3 XOTV, 2 XTCV and 2 XBLV.

Conveys Hull Corporation party, Hull to Wembley Hill and return.

Labelling.—Train to be **side labelled.**

One label to be placed on quarter light of every alternate compartment at each side. The labels must shew time of departure on return journey and all booking stations in geographical order. Spare labels to be handed to guard for renewal of any that become lost or defaced on journey.

HORNSEA SHOW.

No. **29.** **York to Hornsea Bridge—Stock Special "Q."**

		a.m.			p.m.
York	...dep.	8 40	Hornsea Bridge ...	...dep.	6 50
Warthill	...arr.	8 50	Ellerby	...pass	7 0
,, ...	...dep.	9 0	Sutton-on-Hull ...	... ,,	7 10
Pocklington ...	...arr.	9 18	Wilmington ...	... ,,	7 16
,, ...	...dep.	9 28	Hull	...arr.	7 26
Nunburnholme ...	...arr.	9 33	,, ...	...dep.	7 38
,, ...	...dep.	9 43	Cottingham ...	...arr.	7 48
Market Weighton	...arr.	9 50	,, ...	...dep.	7 56
,, ,, ...	...dep.	10 0	Beverley	...arr.	8 4
Beverley	...arr.	10 12	,, ...	...dep.	8 12
,, ...	...dep.	10 20	Market Weighton	...arr.	8 30
Cottingham ...	...arr.	10 28	,, ,, ...	...dep.	8 38
,, ...	...dep.	10 38	Nunburnholme ...	...arr.	8 45
Hull	...arr.	10 46	,, ...	...dep.	8 52
,, ...	...dep.	10 56	Pocklington ...	...arr.	8 57
Wilmington ...	...pass	11 6	,, ...	...dep.	9 5
Sutton-on-Hull ...	... ,,	11 9	Warthill	...arr.	9 20
Ellerby	... ,,	11 21	,, ...	...dep.	9 28
Hornsea Bridge ...	...arr.	11 30	York	...arr.	9 38

Stock—2 B.

to Scarborough, Sunday arrivals in Hull were at 12.10 p.m. and 8.11 p.m., both missing Cayton.

There was a good service of fourteen trains to Hornsea before 1914, with two trains on Sundays. The best were two fast trains taking the commuters home from Hull during the week, that at 5.18 p.m. running non stop and getting to Hornsea at 5.45 with conditional stops at Wilmington and Hornsea Bridge, followed by the 5.50 p.m. which arrived at 6.20 including three stops on the way. These trains were matched by the 8.50 a.m. Up train which ran non stop to Hull, reached at 9.18. The Sunday trains were one out and home morning and afternoon to give scope for a day's outing, calling at all stations except Wassand, rather a jokey sort of place which had only one train stopping in each direction on Mondays only. Withernsea fared similarly, though with slightly less weekday trains at eleven and similar Sunday out and home trains. The express run for returning coastal commuters left Hull at 5.23 p.m., stopping only at Southcoates, to reach Withernsea at 6.00 p.m. which also halted at Southcoates. Again, the Sunday trains were balanced to provide a decent day outing if required.

Sundays 1914

Hull	dep:	8.00a.m.	7.45a.m.	3.58p.m.	4.57p.m.
Hornsea	arr:	8.47	"	4.43	"
Withernsea	arr:	"	8.41	"	5.43
Withernsea	dep:	"	9.00a.m.	"	5.16p.m.
Hornsea	dep:	9.00a.m.	"	4.57p.m.	"
Hull	arr:	9.46	9.56	5.43	6.13

In 1942 the Hornsea trains were nine or ten in number, with none of them attaining the status of express; the overall running time was about 45 minutes. Wassand had disappeared off the timetable, though was retained as a footnote whereby the 4.20 p.m. from Hull could set down and the 10.55 a.m. from Hornsea could take up. How many folk were around to take up the facility, one wonders? Possibly, as it was for Mondays only, it was to enable some wifely soul to up sticks and fly into Hull to escape the rigours of washday! The Sunday trains were again turn abouts and were by now probably a 'Sentinel' railcar making two round trips.

The pattern of Withernsea services was almost identical to that for Hornsea, even to the Sunday services worked by railcar. The Withernsea service on Sundays left Hull at 8.05 a.m. and 7.05 p.m., followed by the Hornsea one at 8.15 a.m. and 7.10 p.m., so that anyone waiting at a wayside station would need his or her wits about them to catch the right one.

After the end of hostilities it was time to restore some of what had been

Cherry Tree crossing, Beverley, with a Class A8 4-6-2T passing on a Bridlington train. C. T. Goode

lost before, and the railways also had Nationalisation to cope with in 1948, which brought some initial benefits and a rush of often enterprising services helped by Thompson's B1 class 4-6-0s on the old LNER section. There were still two through services to King's Cross, the 8.45 a.m. which reached London at 1.05 p.m., and the 'Yorkshire Pullman' at 10.40 a.m., a revival of the pre-war service which commenced in 1935 when it was decided to stop the train at Doncaster to attach and detach a portion for Hull. This gave the city a 3½ hour service to and from London for the first time in its history, and led to a splendid piece of main line running whereby the 4.45 p.m. return from the capital had to run the 156 miles in 156 minutes, and the Up service in one minutes less, headed by one of the older ex GN C1 class 'Atlantics'.

After the war the portion of three cars was run to Doncaster by a D49, K3 or similar and attached to the front of the Leeds and Bradford cars by the main train engine, while on return to Doncaster the Leeds section left ahead of the Hull cars which were left rather forlornly in the platform for collection by the Hull men. Timings were not very good for days out in London, as the Up service did not reach there until 2.42 p.m. On Saturdays an extra through train left Hull at 8.10 a.m., reaching London at 12.30 p.m. Trains directly to Hull from King's Cross were more generous, though complicated, with arrivals at 12.57 p.m., 3.08 or 3.28 p.m., depending on the day, 6.27 p.m. which had through coaches to Bridlington, the Pullman in at 9.26 p.m. and the 11.09 p.m. which was earlier on Fris. and Sats. On Saturdays a train arrived at 12.38 p.m., the whole going forward to Filey Holiday camp. A summer Saturday train also came from London at 2.36 p.m. On Sundays there were two services through to the capital, at 10.00, arrive at 2.50 p.m. and at 2.28 p.m., arrive at 7.10 p.m., the latter leaving Bridlington at 1.15 p.m. Sunday arrivals in Hull were at 3.25 and 6.23 p.m.

The old GC route to Liverpool via Sheffield and Manchester saw departures at 9.20 a.m. from Hull, arriving Liverpool Cen. at 12.40 p.m., as well as the 4.05 p.m. which reached Liverpool at 8.57 p.m. This train stopped also at Hessle and Ferriby for some reason on the way out. The incoming service arrived at 2.16 and 9.04 p.m. Both services ran more or less to the same pattern on Sundays. The L & Y service left at 1.15 p.m. and returned at 6.35 p.m. with the added zest on Fridays only of a run to Manchester during the high season, arriving at 9.17 p.m. One interesting development as a result of amalgamation was a new service from Hull to Sheffield Midland ahead of the old GC one to Liverpool, which ran on to the old LMS section via the Swinton curve, as do the modern workings exclusively. This was due in Sheffield at 11.02 a.m. and after the engine, usually a Botanic Gardens D49 had had a good rest, returned at 3.45 p.m. to reach Hull at 5.40 p.m. The powers-that-be were wont to experiment with this service sometimes, often at short notice, when it would be advertised as extended to run through to Derby, Birmingham or even Bristol. The Hull engine had spare time to take the train on, but whether it actually did so is not known. In the fifties a Fridays only train was booked in the season, this time Midland in origin, to run overnight from Hull to Bristol for benefit of incipient holidaymakers. The train had arrived earlier in Hull on a working from Sheffield.

First impressions of the later trains offered to Leeds are of rather a hotch-potch, with five all-stations slows mixed with in with odd expresses and extra Saturday trains. There were three through services to Liverpool Lime St.. at 9.00 a.m., 2.00 and 4.00 p.m. getting in at 12.37, 5.50 and 7.56 p.m. respectively, while the first curiosity was a Saturday morning 7.50 a.m. to Blackpool Cen. (arr. 12.47 p.m.) which doubled as a slow train, stopping almost everywhere to Leeds first of all. Then came the 8.35 a.m. Saturday non stop to Selby, then on to Manchester Exchange (arr: 11.10 a.m.) and the 10.45 a.m., also Saturdays for Bradford Forster Sq. (arr. 12.57 p.m.) which also ran non stop to Selby. Brough was obviously out of favour in 1950! This comment is reinforced by the 1.05 p.m. also fast to Leeds though with Brough stops, while at 8.35 p.m., also on Sundays, a relic of the old days ran in the shape of the train to Selby which divided for Pontefract and Leeds. On Sundays there was a 7.00 a.m. and 7.00 p.m. slow and five expresses to Selby, one of which, the 6.45 p.m. went on to York, arrival at 7.55 p.m. The return was from York at 9.38 p.m., arriving back at 11.05 p.m.

An early service ran at 3.35 a.m. from York on weekdays, arriving in

Photo-call for LMS visitor to Dairycoates, 2P No. 586 in 1930. *Coll: C. T. Goode*

Hull at 4.37 a.m. The inbound Liverpool trains arrived in Hull at 2.50 and 7.51 p.m., while the star turn was the 11.40 a.m. SO from Manchester Exchange which, after leaving Leeds at 1.22 p.m., ran non stop to Hull which it reached at 2.42 p.m. There was a return arrival from Bradford Forster Square at 5.09 p.m. Fastest of the Sunday trains into Hull were the 3.20 a.m., in at 4.29 a.m. and the 1.00 p.m. in at 2.15 p.m. In these days 75 minutes for 52 miles, including the Selby stop and the slowing for the swing bridge was a good performance.

The train service on the Hornsea line latterly was much the same as hitherto, with eleven or twelve trains, including the fast departure from Hull as 5.18 p.m. which had but three stops, and equivalent 8.28 a.m. from Hornsea, due in Hull at 9.05 a.m. The joker station of Wassand still featured, with one morning train halting in the Hull direction on Mondays, then a halt for a Hornsea bound train in the afternoon. There were four services on Sundays, one, the 10.15 a.m. being fast and leaving Hornsea, also express, at 6.15 p.m.

The complementary service to Withernsea had the same number of trains on offer, but with fast trains leaving Hull at 5.50 and 6.35 a.m., the latter non stop to Rye Hill & Burstwick which sounds as if it might have been chosen out of a hat, and one at 5.27 p.m. timed out just after the Hornsea flyer. At 9.20 a.m. there was an interesting run to Marfleet only which ran to puzzle the researcher, since it is not shown as returning. Such cases do arise and are explained either by the company allowing the rolling stock to pile up in the sidings or, what is more likely, to either run home empty or attach vehicles to other trains. Commuters into Hull had the 8.18 a.m. from Withernsea which reached Hull at 8.54, the only sparkling service of the day. On Sundays there were five trains, two of which, the 9.35 and 10.35 a.m. collected everybody as far as Marfleet then ran fast, returning similarly at 6.05 and 7.05 p.m., preceded by a fast service at 5.05 p.m.; obviously someone was trying out the idea of a regular interval service.

The independent Hull & Barnsley passenger timetable was, by comparison with all the foregoing, quite modest, dividing neatly into the main services between Hull and Cudworth which were extended to Sheffield Mid. in 1905, those to Knottingley on the L & Y via Carlton and locals out to South Cave or Howden. After the beginning of 1932 no passenger trains ran west of South Howden, and these continued until August 1955. In 1899 there were eight trains to Cudworth on weekdays, all slow and taking about one hour forty minutes, except the 9.25 a.m. and the even faster 11.40 a.m. which stopped only at Howden before Kirk Smeaton and reached Cudworth at 1.00 p.m. with a connection for Sheffield, arriving there at 2.05 p.m. On Sundays there was one train only through to Cudworth at 10.00 a.m. On weekdays there were two through trains to Knottingley and one on Sundays. The other way, there were seven trains the whole length of the line and three from Knottingley, the best express, which ran on Sundays also, being the 5.05 a.m. from Cudworth which stopped at Howden and reached Cannon Street at 6.25 a.m. All trains stopped at Beverley Road. To leaven things, there were a couple of turn about runs out to North Cave.

The H & B had for several years been interested in the idea of reaching Sheffield and tried various schemes without success. In 1904, however, an agreement was made with the Midland Railway for running powers from Cudworth to Sheffield. This was fine, except that the H & B had no suitable carriages immediately available, nor a decent reception at Cannon Street for the passengers it was certain would come flooding in. The Midland, therefore offered the loan of some coaches during the winter of 1905, due for return by the following April. And so, from 2nd. October 1905 a service began, using three borrowed six -wheelers, as follows:

Cannon Street	dep:	9.15a.m.	12.45p.m.	2.45	5.05
Sheffield	arr:	10.59	2.25	4.24	6.50
Sheffield	dep:	10.00	12.50	4.28	8.22
Cannon Street	arr:	11.50	2.35	6.10	10.00

One set of coaches was stabled in Sheffield overnight, and the engine would run light to and from Cudworth shed each morning and night, a fair mileage. After the return of the Midland stock the trains made do with old H & B four wheelers until new corridor vehicles appeared in 1907, and one of the middle trains of the day was taken off. A Sunday train was put on with the advent of the new stock, leaving Hull at 1.25 p.m. arrive Sheffield at 3.26 p.m. and starting back at 7.52 p.m. for an arrival at 9.50 p.m. The services were running at a loss and economies were made by cutting down on the slower trains and allowing the faster ones more stops; the Knottingley service was also reduced.

By October 1910 the Sheffield trains were three in number and with the additional stops at each station out to North Cave; indeed, one train stopped everywhere right through, the idea of a smart, fast service was destroyed, though timings were still optimistic:

Cannon Street	dep:	9.40a.m.	12.30p.m.	5.00
Sheffield	arr:	11.45	3.08	6.55
Sheffield	dep:	7.30a.m.	2.03p.m.	6.58
Cannon Street	arr:	9.45	4.10	9.18

There was no longer a Sunday train. Local stations such as Willerby did well out of the arrangements, with twelve trains stopping in each direction and four on Sundays:

Willerby Weekdays (Trains for Hull):

8.31 a.m.	1.25 p.m.	6.58 p.m.
9.32	2.54 (Tues & Thurs)	9.12
11.34	4.04	10.14
	5.12	10.28
	6.04	

(Trains westbound):

6.12a.m.	Howden	12.34p.m.	Sheffield
7.04	Cudworth	1.29	Howden (Tues & Thurs)
9.44	Sheffield	3.04	Sheffield
11.04	Knottingley	4.09	North Cave
		5.49	North Cave
		7.04	Cudworth
		9.04	North Cave
		11.04	Cudworth.

Sundays for Hull: 2.20p.m., 6.01, 6.51, 8.51, 10.34

(Trains westbound):

1.42a.m.	Cudworth	1.28p.m.	North Cave
		3.13	Knottingley

Towards the end of the Great War the timetable showed only two trains each way between Hull and Cudworth, three as far as Howden and four to North Cave; nine departures in all from Hull. On Sundays there was one run each way between Hull and Cudworth. The Sheffield service had disappeared for good, though not before producing a little competition from the NER who, in 1910 tried through service of its own to Sheffield Midland with two trains daily leaving Hull at 9.38 a.m. and 3.20 p.m., and Sheffield at 9.42 a.m. and 5.10 p.m. The running time was 105 minutes, which beat the H & B effort hand down.

After amalgamation with the NER in 1922 the service ran as before for several years, except that after 13th. July 1924 the trains were diverted down the new link to reach Paragon station, and Cannon Street was closed. The last train had left there at 10.40 a.m. (Sunday) and returned at 5.55 p.m. Mr. F. A. Richardson, who had issued the first ticket when the station had opened on 27th. July 1885, issued the last one in his final role as Station Master. Mentioning tickets reminds of the joke long current around the railways in the area that the H & B was so poor that it used to use the same tickets over and over again by reissuing those collected at the barriers-a primitive form of re-cycling.

Railcar experiments

On 12th. March 1928 an improved 'Sentinel' steam railcar was tried between Hull and South Howden and was the first of an era of use, not

"Sentinel" railcar 'Cleveland' at Beverley in 1931. *T. Rounthwaite*

always successful, however. From 8th. April 1929, in answer to road competition, local lines round Hull were put on a regular interval basis, with H & B trains leaving at five minutes to the hour, resulting in between 17 to 20 trains in each direction. There were still the odd runs to Cudworth, including the one Sunday train, but these were withdrawn from 1st. January 1932 and the main line closed on Sundays.

Mention of the regular interval services tempts one to mention the others, along with their instrument, namely the perky and interesting 'Sentinel' railcars which invaded the old NER territory like a benevolent plague at this time. The other regular departures from Hull were to Brough at 15 minutes past and Beverley at 15 minutes to the hour, serviced by the largest allocation to the area at Botanic Gardens. Each car had a stage coach name; in this case Hull had 'Valliant', 'Tally Ho', 'Rockingham', 'High Flyer', 'True Briton', 'Celerity', 'Cornwallis', 'Teazle', 'Trafalgar', 'Eclipse' and 'Yorkshire Huzzar', all available for scuttling about, getting as far as Goole or Thorne North, Withernsea and South Howden, with short runs to Beverley and Brough thrown in. There were occasional runs to Bridlington, especially with the 5.10 a.m. which ran non stop and took just one hour, getting on station for the fast 6.25 a.m. back to Hull, calling at Beverley to pick up a trailer. Hornsea saw railcars chiefly on Sats. only.

Bridlington had its own railcar 'Criterion' which worked two trips to Selby via Driffield. On Wednesday only around 1933 the railcar did an extra service leaving Bridlington at 8.45 p.m. all stations to Hull, returning at 10.50 p.m., running fast and arriving back in Bridlington at 11.46 p.m. The Saturday 10.50 p.m. was often lightly loaded and therefore given to a 'Sentinel'.

Selby shed had originally two cars, 'Cleveland' and 'Surprise' which busied themselves on the Goole branch and with local runs to Wressle and Holme Moor. However, on Mondays a car ran empty to Leeds at 5.05 a.m. to form the 6.00 Leeds-Brough for aircraft factory workers who lived in Leeds and commuted daily. This arrived at Brough at 7.22 a.m., then ran empty to Staddlethorpe to form the 7.38 from there to Goole and the 7.57 Goole to Selby, a good early example of cyclic working in 1932.

The railcars performed up to and during the 1939-45 war, though becoming more and more decrepit and unreliable, which was not helped in some cases by the application of wartime brown paint. An old D17 4-4-0, equally doddery, would be put on the service with one or two coaches if a car should fail, and it was disappointing to turn up at somewhere like Selby in the hope of a railcar ride out to Drax Hales and back to find a replacement panting away at the platform. The last steam railcar went from Botanic Gardens, 'Recovery', and 'Integrity' from Selby in November 1947. When war broke out the H & B was busy with its coal and freight, but lost all its Howden trains except two, though these improved again after 6th. October 1941 when push and pull trains worked by G5 0-4-4s came to work the line up to the end of passenger traffic on 30th. July

TIME-TABLE OF TRAINS BETWEEN

HULL, HENSALL (for Lancashire & Yorkshire Railway), and CUDWORTH (for Midland Railway).

All Trains are 1st, 2nd, and 3rd Class, on Hull and Barnsley Railway.

This Time Table shows the Times at which the Trains may be expected to arrive at and depart from the several Stations. But their departure or arrival at the times stated is not guaranteed, nor does the Company hold itself responsible for delay or any consequences arising therefrom. The granting of Tickets to Passengers to places off the Company's Lines is an arrangement made for the greater convenience of the Public, but the Company does not hold itself responsible for any delay, detention, or other loss or injury whatsoever, arising off its Lines, or from the act or defaults of other parties, nor for the correctness of the Times so far as they relate to the Lines of other Companies, nor for the arrival of this Company's own Trains passing over one portion of the Line in time for the nominally corresponding Trains on the other portion of their own Lines, or on the Lines of any other Company or Party.

JULY 27TH, 1885, AND UNTIL FURTHER NOTICE.

FROM HULL		WEEK-DAYS.														SUNDAYS.			
		a.m.	a.m.	a.m.	a.m.	a.m.	a.m.	p.m.	p.m.	p.m.	p.m.	p.m.	p.m.	p.m.	p.m.	a.m.	p.m.	p.m.	p.m.
Hull, Barnsley, and West Riding Junction Railway.																			
HULL { Cannon Street	dep.	6 5	7 10	8 15	8 40	10 45	11 30	12 55	1 20		3 5	4 40	5 0	6 30	9 15	9 0	12 50	3 20	7 0
HULL { Beverley Road	..	6 8	7 13	8 18	8 43	10 48	11 33	12 58	1 23		3 8	4 43	5 3	6 33	9 18	9 3	12 53	3 23	7 3
Willerby and Kirk Ella	..	6 20	7 24	8 30		11 0	..	1 10			3 19	4 55		6 45	9 30	9 15	1 4	3 35	7 15
Little Weighton	..	6 29	7 32	8 39	..	11 9		1 19			3 27	5 4		6 54	9 39	9 24	1 12	3 44	7 4
South Cave	..	6 40	7 42	8 50		11 20	11 59	1 30			3 37	5 15	5 28	7 5	9 50	9 35	1 22	3 55	7 25
North Cave	..	6 45	7 46	8 55		11 25		1 35			3 41	5 20	..	7 10			1 26	4 0	
Newport (Yorks)	..	6 53	7 53	9 3	..	11 33		1 43			3 48			7 18			1 33	4 8	
Sandholme	..	6 57	7 57	9 7	..	11 37	..	1 47			3 52			7 22	..	..	1 37	4 12	..
Eastrington	..	7 4	8 3	9 14		11 44		1 54			3 58			7 29			1 43	4 19	
HOWDEN	..	7 12	8 10	9 22	9 31	11 52	12 23	2 2	2 12	2 25	4 5	5 42	5 52	7 37	..	..	1 50	4 27	..
Drax	..	7 27	8 23	9 37		12 7				2 40	4 18	5 57		7 52			2 3	4 42	
Carlton	..	7 31	8 27	9 41	..	12 11	12 39	..		2 44	4 22	6 1	6 8	7 56	..	..	2 7	4 46	..
Carlton (for L. & Y. R.)	dep.	7 32		9 42		12 12			..	2 45		6 2		7 57				4 47	
Hensall (L. & Y. R.)	arr.	7 43	..	9 53	..	12 23	..	..	..	2 56	..	6 13	..	8 8	..	..	..	4 58	..
L. & Y. Railway.																			
HENSALL	dep.	7 51	..	10 1	..	12 31	..	..	..	3 16		6 21	..	8 16	..	..	..	5 6	..
KNOTTINGLEY	arr.	8 5		10 15		12 45				3 30		[illegible]		8 30				5 20	
PONTEFRACT	,,	8 17	..	10 21	..	12 56	..	..	..	3 36		6 45	..	8 36	..	..		5 30	..
WAKEFIELD	,,	8 42		10 45		1 20				4 2		7 10		9 2				5 55	
LEEDS	,,	[illegible]	..	..	..	1 22	..	..	..		..	7 12	..	..	..	..	..	..	..
H. B. & W. R. J.																			
Kirk Smeaton	dep.	..	8 47	..	..	..	12 59	..	2 47	..	..		6 27	..	..	..	2 27	..	..
Upton and North Elmsall	..		8 57				1 9		2 57				6 37				2 37		
CUDWORTH	arr.		9 13	..	10 28	..	1 24	..	3 12	..	5 3		6 52	..	..	..	2 52	..	..
Midland Railway.																			
CUDWORTH	dep.		9 37		10 40		1 40		3 35		5 30		7 5				3 35		
BARNSLEY	arr.	..	9 47		10 50		1 50	..	3 48	..	5 43	..	7 15	..	..	..	3 45	..	..
CUDWORTH	dep.		9 31		10 38		1 33		3 22		5 11		7 0				2 59		
SHEFFIELD	arr.		10 2	..	11 7	..	2 6	..	3 55	..	5 45	..	7 34	..	..	..	4 3	..	..
SHEFFIELD	dep.		10 6		12 5		2 30		4 18		5 54		7 45				4 10		
DERBY	arr.	..	[illegible]		[illegible]		[illegible]	..	[illegible]		[illegible]	..	[illegible]	..	..	..	[illegible]	..	..
BIRMINGHAM	,,		12 50		2 42		4 55		7 20		8 20		10 25				9 5		
BRISTOL	,,	..	4 0	..	5 20	..	8 0	..	..	..	11 30	..	5 45	..	..	..	5 45	..	..
SHEFFIELD	dep.		10 6		11 30		2 20		4 10		6 20		7 45				4 10		
NOTTINGHAM	arr.	..	11 55	..	12 22	..	3 12	..	5 5	..	7 15	..	9 55	..	..	..	7 15	..	..
LEICESTER	,,		11 50		1 48		4 30		6 20		8 10		10 40				7 27		
LONDON (St. Pancras)	,,	..	2 35	..	3 0	..	5 50	..	7 50	..	10 0	..	2 20	..	..	..	9 45	..	..

TO HULL.

Railway	Station		WEEK-DAYS. a.m.	a.m.	a.m.	a.m.	a.m.	a.m.	p.m.	a.m.	p.m.	p.m.	p.m.	p.m.	p.m.	SUNDAYS. a.m.	p.m.	p.m.	p.m.
Midland Railway.	LONDON (St. Pancras)	dep.				5 15				10 0		12 20			3 40				
	LEICESTER	,,				7 22		9 10		12 0		1 48			6 0				
	NOTTINGHAM	,,				7 35		9 25		12 40		2 55			6 15				
	SHEFFIELD	arr.				8 54		10 48		1 35		3 50			7 36				
	BRISTOL	dep.				1 *3				9 5		10 15			3 5				
	BIRMINGHAM	,,				6 0		8 15		11 40		1 8			5 10				
	DERBY	,,				7 40		9 27		1 25		2 55			6 47				
	SHEFFIELD	arr.				8 54		10 48		2 16		4 5			7 49				
	SHEFFIELD	dep.			7 23	8 58		10 53		2 20		4 12			7 55		2 40		
	CUDWORTH	arr.			3 16	9 29		11 23		2 45		4 43			8 23		3 29		
	BARNSLEY	dep.			8 0	9 15		11 5		2 0		4 5			7 30		2 40		
	CUDWORTH	arr.			8 13	9 25		11 15		2 10		4 15			7 43		2 50		
H. B. & W. R. J.	CUDWORTH	dep.			8 20	9 45		11 30		2 50		4 50			8 30		3 35		
	Upton and North Elmsall	dep.			8 36	10 1		11 46							8 46		[illegible]		
	Kirk Smeaton	,,			8 46			11 56				5 15			8 56		4 2		
L. & Y. Railway.	LEEDS	dep.				9 5			1 8		2 45		6 8	7 35					
	WAKEFIELD	,,		7 30		9 15			1 30		3 15		6 35	7 45					7 40
	PONTEFRACT	,,		7 55		9 40			1 55		3 40		6 54	8 10					8 5
	KNOTTINGLEY	,,		8 2		9 45			2 0		3 45		6 59	8 18					8 20
	HENSALL	arr.		8 16		9 59			2 14		3 59		7 12	8 32					8 24
	Hensall (L. & Y. R.)	dep.		8 20		10 10			2 20		4 5		7 17	8 40					[illegible]
Hull, Barnsley, and West Riding Junction Railway.	Carlton (from L. & Y. R.)	arr.		8 30		10 20			2 30		4 15		7 27	8 50					[illegible]
	Carlton	dep.		8 31	9 6	10 29	10 35		2 31		4 16	5 36	7 28	8 51	9 16		[illegible]		[illegible]
	Drax	,,		8 36	9 10		10 40		2 36		4 21		7 33	8 56	9 21		[illegible]		[illegible]
	HOWDEN	,,		8 51	9 23	10 45	10 56	12 31	2 51	3 48	4 36	5 51	7 48	9 11	9 33		[illegible]		[illegible]
	Eastrington	,,		8 56	9 30		11 3	12 38	2 59		4 44		7 55		9 40		[illegible]		[illegible]
	Sandholme	,,		9 5	9 36		11 10	12 44	3 6		4 51		8 2		9 46		[illegible]		[illegible]
	Newport (Yorks.)	,,		9 9	9 40		11 14	12 48	3 10		4 55		8 6		9 50		[illegible]		[illegible]
	North Cave	,,		9 17	9 47		11 22	12 55	3 18		5 3	6 12	8 14		9 57		[illegible]		[illegible]
	South Cave	,,	7 56	9 22	9 51	11 9	11 27	12 59	3 23		5 8	6 16	8 19	9 30	10 1	[illegible]	[illegible]	[illegible]	[illegible]
	Little Weighton	,,	8 4	9 33	10 1		11 38	1 10	3 34		5 19	6 26	8 29		10 11	[illegible]	[illegible]	[illegible]	[illegible]
	Willerby and Kirk Ella	,,	8 11	9 42	10 9		11 47	1 18	3 43		5 28	6 34	8 38	9 58	10 19	[illegible]	[illegible]	[illegible]	[illegible]
	HULL { Beverley Road	,,	8 21	9 54	10 20	11 35	12 0	1 30	3 55	4 36	5 40	6 45	8 50	10 10	10 30	[illegible]	[illegible]	[illegible]	[illegible]
	HULL { Cannon Street	arr.	8 25	9 58	10 25	11 40	12 5	1 35	4 0	4 40	5 45	6 50	8 55	10 15	10 35	[illegible]	[illegible]	[illegible]	[illegible]

* Does not start from Bristol on Monday Morning.

RETURN TICKETS are available as follows: { For distances not exceeding 12 miles—Day of issue or following day. ,, ,, above 12 and not exceeding 80 miles—Seven Days. ,, ,, ,, 80 miles—One Month.

HULL, JULY 22ND, 1885. V. W. HILL, Tra[illegible]

Large Boilered C1 'Atlantic' on 'Yorkshire Pullman' at Hessle. *T. Rounthwaite*

1955, when No. 67337 pushed the 8.30 p.m. out of Paragon and left Howden on the 10.30 return. This last train had been rather curious at one time in that it was booked to South Cave, then ran empty to North Cave where it was left for the night to form the first morning service. However, passengers were allowed to use it if travelling to North Cave. One assumes that the engine ran back light to Hull.

In 1953 a lightweight diesel unit was tried on the line, and in 1954 a summer excursion to Bridlington from South Howden was run with some success and featured each year up to 1958, hauled by an A5 tank locomotive. There had been odd excursions earlier over the H & B, chiefly to Hull Fair, though B1 No. 61085 took a football excursion from Kirk Smeaton to Leeds on 28th. February 1953.

Engines on passenger services included the aforementioned A5 latterly, preceded by ex GN C12 4-4-2Ts. old H & B 0-6-0 types, the NER A8 and J27 types and even a Q6 0-8-0 goods engine in one instance which, it is hoped, had a pump for the air brakes!

After 1922 goods trains were worked by ex H & B 0-8-0s which were evidently unpopular even with the company's own men, with the result that the more powerful NE Q6s and ex GC 2-8-0s more or less took over operations. After the war, and until the last through coal train ran on 29th.

November 1959, hauled by No. 90352, the freight had been handled by the ubiquitous WD 2-8-0s which seemed to thrive on indifference and neglect. The H & B main line was cut back, first to Carlton, then to Little Weighton, with a daily pick-up train running out from Neptune Street to keep the signalmen en route in occupation, one suspects. Even this had its moments when the shed laid on something exotic to run the odd wagon or two plus brake van; once or twice a B1 or D49, on one occasion a 'Jubilee' which was ostensibly being tested after repairs carried out following failure on an excursion. Springhead had closed in December 1958, so that the guest artists would have emanated from Dairycoates. The Neptune Street branch was closed in 1962 and the final closure of the main line from Springhead to Little Weighton closed on 6th. July 1964.

Locomotives used

To try to mention every type of locomotive which visited Hull over the years would be impossible and certainly very tedious, except to a few diehards. Initially there were a wide range of NER classes intermingled with 'foreign' engines making an appearance, as several Johnson 2-4-0s of the MR were based in Hull for that company's trains out to Milford Jc. to connect with the York-Sheffield trains. The MS & L had one of their Sacré 4-4-0s shedded in Hull for the Liverpool service as did the LNWR mentioned earlier. Initially there were the NER Fletcher varieties, then the Worsdell machines, such as the 'Waterburys', so called after an accurate pocket watch of the day. These handled the expresses, and the G5 tanks which covered the humdrum workings up to the end of steam. The LNER had a shot at developing the Hull-Tyne link, with a new express service from Newcastle at 12.10 p.m., reversing at York and arriving in Hull at 3.17 p.m. with a return at 4.47p.m. Hull turned out a 4-4-0 of the D20 class on the run, either No. 1239/40 or 45/6. The later Gresley K3s were tried but not regularly used. The last Class X single drivers were in use around Hull until 1935, the area forming a last resting place for items of rolling stock on their last legs. Thus the use of older 4-4-0s, then the C6 and C7 'Atlantics' retired from main line duties for newer Gresley types; the Cs had a run or two with the Liverpool trains in wartime and, though often smart externally, let the side down by stalling with trains which were just too heavy for them.

A big change of policy came with the advert of the D49 Class 4-4-0s which came to Hull as new engines to handle the expresses, first the 'Shires', then the 'Hunts'. There were, latterly, 12 D49s at Botanic Gardens, some of which had been there all their days and which still managed turn on the 'Yorkshire Pullman' and Sheffield workings up to 1960. For express freight work there were the K3s, stout 2-6-0s which also performed well on passenger services.

The G5 tanks were augmented by A8 4-6-2Ts (Springhead had a few inferior A7s for general use) and A5 tanks from Darlington which had an unmistakable GC flavour to them. From Cleveland came an exchange of L1 2-6-4Ts during winter, with the A8s, but back they went in the summer season to work the Middlesbrough-Scarborough trains. In 1956 the L1s were replaced by V1 and V3 2-6-2Ts which were used on services to York, Scarborough and Doncaster. During the early sixties the Ivatt 2-6-0, an ugly beast, was seen on H & B services, while old GN 4-4-0s of classes D2 and 3 were around for a time. Back in the thirties the old GN classes C1 and 2 'Atlantic's', including the only one bearing a name, 'Henry Oakley', came in as foreigners from Sheffield, as did the GC 'Directors' and other 4-4-0 types, the larger GC 4-6-0s from Sheffield and Mexborough.

'Henry Oakley' was at Mexborough for quite a time in the thirties and spent much of it at Botanic Gardens when on runs to Hull. His schedule between 1930 and 1936 is as follows:

8.41a.m.	Mexborough to Hull	3.40	Express Sheffield-Hull (London coaches attached at Doncaster)
11.55	Slow Hull-Doncaster	9.18	Slow Hull-Doncaster
1.45p.m.	Slow Doncaster-Sheffield	10.55	Doncaster-Mexborough

"Henry Oakley" at Botanic, with ex NE Class D21 4-4-0 behind. *T. Rounthwaite*

Two sets of men were on the turn. C1 No. 3254 was the other engine used on the roster.

The Thompson B1s and WD 2-8-0s largely took over everything in the end, but a nice finale to the chapter of GC working into Hull was a Friday in Spring 1957 when a 'Director' ran into the city on the express from Liverpool. 'Marne' it was, at the time when a visit to Sheffield would reveal several of the class either lying up outside Darnall shed or used for carriage shunting. Apparently the rostered B1 had failed and the driver, himself due for retirement, had begged the shed foreman to be allowed to take the engine out for a run to Hull in its place. Good nature prevailed, and there she was, waiting to take the 4.13 p.m. out, with buffet car and all!

Latter use of ex LMS types were the Fowler 2-6-2Ts sent in 1956 as replacements for G5s but soon returned, and Standard Class 2 No. 84009 of Royston shed which was borrowed for a time. The latter shed also sent Class 4F 0-6-0s and 8F 2-8-0s down the H & B on coal trains from time to time. Once daily, Wakefield L & Y shed sent an engine on a passenger working, at first a 2P 4-4-0, then a 2-6-4T, often No. 42477.

A brief mention now of the Armstrong trails-Whitworth Sulzer engined diesel unit 'Lady Hamilton' which entered service after exhaustive trails in June 1934, going to Botanic Gardens and taking up a Hull diagram of return runs to Pontefract, Selby, York and back to Pontefract and return in the same day. The lady proved fickle and the X2 2-2-4T at Hull to work the District Engineers saloon, No. 957 was used to work things instead. Sometimes a spare D20 was pressed into use. Whatever it was, the assemblage had to get to York in 52 minutes and return after a mere half an hour break. In 1935, D17s Nos. 1871/3 from West Hartlepool took over.

'Lady Hamilton' worked less than half of its booked times and spent a lot in Darlington Works. In 1939 it was given lighter duties to Beverley, Brough and South Howden, and was withdrawn in December 1939. In February 1936 'Northumbrian', a similar vehicle, was transferred from Leeds to Hull as a standby and did much of the Lady's work without major ado. However, upon its next general repair, in May 1939, 'Northumbrian' was withdrawn. The name 'Lady Hamilton' was chosen lightly by an employee at the builder's as the northern answer to 'Lord Nelson' on the Southern Railway, over which the car was in fact tested for a time.

In the early thirties a curiosity appeared on the 3.20 p.m. goods from York, in the shape of the Kitson-Still steam-diesel locomotive which was a big, ungainly 2-6-2T built by Kitson of Leeds in 1927 with the pull of a steam engine and economy of a diesel. Steam started it off, before the diesel power took over above 6 mph., though both forces could work on gradients. What with this, 'Lady Hamilton' and X class engines, the scene was certainly varied in quality!

Dairycoates, once one of the largest sheds in the region with three roundhouses, found itself at the end with one, plus an open turntable and with all the freight workings and western dock shunting. It provided power for summer Saturday workings to and from the coast resorts, for which a supply of K3 and B1s was available. One B1 was rostered for Blackpool via Wakefield There were LMR 2-6-0s used for specials out to the halt at Boothferry Park, opened near Springbank South in 1951, and WDs to work as far as Crewe, Sheffield and Scarborough. Foreign freight visitors were 9F 2-10-0s and various ex LNER 2-8-0s and J6s, plus Fowler 0-8-0s off the LMS through Goole.

Botanic Gardens was closed in 1959 to clear the site for a new diesel depot, with remaining steam stock stored outside the station before taking up trains and living at Dairycoates. In 1950 the shed was host to 50 resident engines, including five B1s, three D20s, 13 D49s, five G5s and sundry others, including one Y1 'Sentinel' shunter. The really impressive express locomotives seldom visited Hull either to stay or as visitors, but an exception was the use of an A3 'Pacific' from Neville Hill which took out the 9a.m. Liverpool. One was more likely to see a 'Pacific' or a V2 on a freight from York, though excursions have more recently brought in a 'Britannia' or two on occasion.

Springhead shed survived quite well, first the general run-down, then the occupation by the Admiralty during the last war. Latterly it was given up almost exclusively to WDs, J 73 tanks and 350 hp. diesel shunters. The last three A7 tanks were scrapped from here. While Botanic Gardens was being converted to a diesel depot, Springhead was used to store rows of D49 and B16 locos. pending withdrawal, and also the new dmus. A sub-shed to Springhead was Alexandra Dock, a two road wooden affair which was closed in 1927, leaving the goodly assortment of tank engines out in the open. In 1950 there were 24 engines living here which were employed on shuffling merchandise round the docks; if they moved further afield they were recognisable by the trip numbers which they carried. Steam had gone by 1960 and 350 hp. and 200 hp. diesel shunters had replaced it. Bigger engines were to be found on trip duties, such as A7s, N8s, 9s and 10s and elderly 0-6-0s. Rather oddly, the B16 4-6-0 was never shedded in Hull for long periods, even though it was a popular visitor on excursion and freight workings from elsewhere. The large T1 4-8-2Ts were employed on banking work in New Inward Yard exclusively until 1952, when the diesels arrived; thereafter they were moved to York and Tyne Dock. On Nationalisation and the establishment of shed codes, Dairycoates became the Hull area HQ as 53A, Botanic Gardens 53B and Springhead 53C. For the record, Bridlington was 53D and Goole 53E. When the area was 'rationalised' and the Hull district disbanded, York became 50A, with Dairycoates 50B and Botanic 50C, though as this took place in 1960, the latter is only theoretical.

Locomotives to be found at Dairycoates in 1960 were as follows:

 B1: 61010/12 61065 61080 61215 61256 61305/6

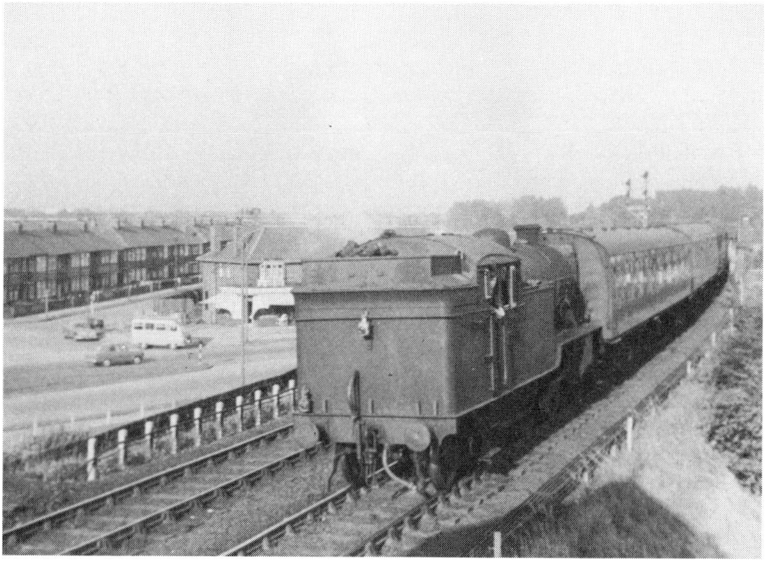

Class V1 No. 67624 on the H & B lines with a football special at Springbank South.
M. Haddon

K3: 61813/4 61819 61846/7 61857 61869/71/2 61874/5 61892/361897-1904 61920 61922/3 61927 61932/5 61941 61945 61965 61985
D49: 62723/7 62729/63/65 62712 J39: 64709 64819/31 64971
J25: 65691/3 V1: 67635/8/40 67663/7 67682/4/6 J94: 68042
J72: 68672 68716/45 L1: 69009/10 Class 2: 84009
WD: 90006/8/9/30/78/99 90217/272/352/378/427/450/482 90571/586/623 90627/670/677/688 90695.

The 'straight line' between Hessle Road Jc. and Cottingham South was used until its closure to carry summer passenger trains and Saturday services between King's Cross and Filey Holiday camp, which also had direct runs to and from Sheffield and Manchester Victoria and Birmingham. There were services to Bridlington from Sheffield, Rotherham and Bradford, and to Scarborough from the Nottingham area. Perversely, perhaps, came a through service from Blackpool and stations en route, worked by a Class 5, though sometimes with a Blackpool 'Jubilee'.

The Diesel era

The exploits of the early diesel units is now of course history, so some record must be set down about them here. First in the post-war field was the ACV four wheeled unit which came for trials on Hull local services, from 6th. July to 25th. July 1953; it replaced a Botanic G5 0-4-4T with runs to Beverley, Brough and South Howden, some 167 miles in all. Comments appear to have been favourable, though the riding must have been rough, if today's 'Pacers', supposedly the latest yell, are anything to go by. On 9th. August 1956 the first Cravens two car unit arrived for crew training, running locally everywhere except on the H & B, much to the annoyance of those who had recently lost their passenger trains. By 1st. January 1957 other units had arrived, eight in all, to take over some of the runs to Withernsea, Hornsea, Brough and Goole. On 4th. March more units arrived and additional services were replaced. Summer brought the units to Bridlington and one train to Scarborough, while more appeared in the 1957-8 winter timetable, with complete transfer of the York service. Odd Bridlington trains remained steamhauled to cope with such traffic as horse boxes collected from the sidings at Burton Agnes which required a shunt and a tail load from time to time.

NER 'Diesel Day' was 5th. January 1959, by which time 31 Cravens twin units were available, some already rather rattly round the windows. These were added to by a number of Birmingham RCW four car units, of a more robust design; these took over most of the Leeds services, apart from the Liverpool and some rush hour trains. The service was improved and more reliable and worked hourly between nine and five p.m. Almost everything was now dieselised and units now ran to Doncaster and Sheffield, with additional services to Sheffield Midland worked by Sheffield units. There were at times some oddities, such as a morning service to Hull worked by a unit from Pye Bridge between Trent and Chesterfield, departing at around 10.00 a.m., and a through dmu working from Hull to Bradford Exchange via Wakefield. The author's hour of glory was to hire a new two car unit for a run to Hexham from Hull with a school party around 1960. This ran non stop each way, apart from reversal and checking at York. Probably a record for the period, one would imagine, with a return trip of 288 miles involved.

On 2nd. January 1961 the 'Inter-City' units arrived on the trans-pennine service to Liverpool, which really transformed matters, giving a regular service of fast and comfortable trains, though one had a feeling that the interiors with their soft furnishings and dark panelling were dated from the outset. The engines, too, tended to be temperamental at times and units were often subject to delay at Leeds while fitters had to be found to tinker somewhere beneath them. The first set due out to Liverpool at 9.00 a.m. had a pre-run on an early round trip to Beverley with Armstrong's factory workers, just to make sure that all was present and in working order!

During the first week passenger revenue at Hull and Huddersfield increased by 30% and by 40% at Leeds, as might be expected. There were five express runs between Hull and Liverpool each way, interspersed with a service from Newcastle to Liverpool at Leeds, giving a regular interval service from the latter station at 15 minutes to each hour, and from Liverpool on the hour for much of the day. The units were made up to six cars in service, the total order being 34 power cars and 17 trailers, built at the BR Swindon works. In each rake were four power cars giving 1,840 hp. from BUT Leyland engines, seating for 60 first and 232 second class and a griddle buffet car. One of the sets was last seen in an unseemly condition at Sheffield Midland, finishing its days on a very slow service to New Mills.

The services to King's Cross have been traced already initially there were four through trains each day, then two and later three. Some difficulty has in the past stemmed from an attitude that Hull is at the end of the branch, which was sometimes felt by a passenger at Doncaster when confronted by the sight of the hurriedly departing train for Hull which had not awaited the connection. Things seen to be planned much better nowadays. One redundant 'Midland Pullman' set did arrive for training purposes in the sixties, but after a time nothing further was heard.

The Freight scene

Freight traffic has declined, as elsewhere, and Hull of course depends on what passes through the port. Fish has more or less vanished as a commodity, and the trains which used to rush through Hessle in the late afternoon, pursued by that rare aroma are no more. At one time the LNER handled 65% of all fish landed in Britain, and Hull 25% of it. In the sixties there were eight trains from Hull each day, five on Saturdays, running to Plymouth, Leeds, King's Cross, Banbury, Manchester, Guide Bridge and Normanton. These were then reduced to three only, to Leeds and Manchester, to Peterborough and London and to the south west via the Midlands. The cuts were due to the reduction in rail traffic demand which caused average train loads of only fifteen vans.

Odd fish vans would be found at the front if to be conveyed right through, or rear if detached en route, of passenger trains, which could lead to some odd looking assemblies on journeys. Fitted freight services left Hull for all parts in the early evening from the Outward yard, for Washwood Heath (Birmingham), Glasgow High St. (the 'Humber-Clyde'), York, Whitemoor (Cambridge) and Ferme Park (London). Inbound trains arrived all day long, in the early hours from King's Cross, then from Manchester, Gateshead and Woodford (Banbury). The Freightliner service for container traffic ran from its own yard at the Hull end of Priory sidings. This site has recently been abandoned to the gypsies and the activities are now concentrated on King George dock.

Coal empties made up the bulk of the forty or so outward freight trains to South Yorkshire collieries, there being a similar influx of wagons at Mineral yard. Mixed freight trains ran to Whitemoor, Colwick, York, Rotherham and Bradford. Seven extra workings appeared after the closure of the H & B line in 1958, these running to and from the collieries via Goole.

Local traffic was not plentiful, though one persistent service was the Hessle Quarry-Wilmington lime traffic, responsibility of the plodding WD 2-8-0s, and a few local pick up trips. Transfer trips from yards to docks and vice-versa tended to depend on the arrival of shipping and not to be part of a fixed timetable, with engines and crews standing by.

Yards on the north side of the running lines, the Inward and Mineral, were developed in 1909 and modernised, as noted earlier. The extension eastwards was known as Priory Yard and was removed again before the original yards. On the south side was the Outward Yard, from which originated the fast goods workings which were transferred to the Inward yard after the former's closure, with the result that these had to travel eastwards to Hessle Road Jc., up the new connection to the old H & B branch as far as Springbank South, then to North Jc., down to Walton Street, round a new spur at Anlaby Road Jc. and back to Hessle Road for right away. The latter traffic was handled by Class 4 diesel engines, to Lawley Street, Whitemoor, Healey Mills, Mottram, Normanton and Glasgow High St. After bickering over rationalisation of the services, much traffic, as with the fish, was lost to road and the yard was left with one service to King's Cross. Coal empties left in the mornings and arrived loaded later in the day.

To reach the above yards, H & B traffic had, in its final days before removal of the Neptune Street branch, to pass along it to the end, then reverse from Neptune St. to pass beneath the NER main line and run past Dairycoates shed.

The end of the level crossings

It was decided to set about eliminating the level crossings in Hull, first of all by removing Hessle Road, which was probably the greatest problem, with 138 closures in seven hours during 1927. As the Neptune St. branch came across at the wrong angle, it was necessary to align it so as to fall into the NER lines over the crossing and also to provided new access to the yards directly, obviating at a stroke the need for trackwork at Neptune Street yard. This was done, along with the removal of two overbridges and the erection of a new power box; then the construction of the new road bridge, or 'Flyover' as such seems to be called hereabouts. One can imagine the difficulties of working in the old signal box under such circumstances for several months. Anlaby Road crossing was replaced in the same way, though here there were hardly the same problems to tackle. A loop was put in here, closed just this year, to enable trains to pass on to or off the Bridlington line without reversal in Hull–in fact it was a replacement for the 'straight line' and, indirectly, the Selby, Market Weighton, Driffield rout. Walton Street was also ear-marked for treatment, but seems to have escaped so far. Possibly there is too much housing close by on the west side to give a run up for a decent bridge here.

Efforts were made to run the Hornsea and Withernsea branches as cheaply as possible by letting guards issue tickets and by de-staffing stations, one of the first areas to try the experiment. It worked well, but did not prevent closure on 19th. October 1964, with the direct York line following on 29th. November 1965, in spite of vigorous opposition in all three cases. The Beaching finger pointed towards the Scarborough line, but here the protests were successful and the axe was stayed.

With closure of the coastal branches it became possible to do something about the other level crossings as all Victoria Dock traffic went round on the low level line, while that from King George Dock and Alexandra Dock passed round the city on the higher level. On 21st. March 1967

Trans-pennine unit passing West Parade in wintry weather. *C. T. Goode*

the Ministry of Transport announced that the British Railways Board could dispose of the low level line, removing frequent delays caused by the six level crossings, in particular Botanic Gardens which had been closing 101 times in four hours during the 1927 survey. Freight services would be diverted to the high level line after certain improvements had been carried out.

On 7th. October 1962 the new electric signal box at Hessle Road was opened, the old crossing closing three weeks earlier. On 2nd. June 1968 the Victoria Dock branch closed and from 1st. May 1968 Hessle Road took control of signalling as far as the manual Alexandra Dock cabin.

The Hessle-Wilmington lime traffic was at first worked over the H & B to the east and back over the Victoria dock line to Southcoates until a connection was put in at Burleigh Street from the H & B to the Hornsea branch, opened in October 1968. Traffic could now reach the cement works by reversing, a routine which carried on until 5th. January 1976, when the siding closed, and presumably the traffic ceased.

H & B lines between Alexandra Dock and King George Dock closed in September 1973 and all traffic was diverted to the NER lines. Alexandra Dock signal box closed on 27th. May 1974. The actual dock had closed in 1982, but after the abolition of the dock labour scheme, a revival of trade followed and it reopened on 16th. July 1991, 106 years to the day after its original opening.

Riverside Quay and emigrants

Riverside Quay was put into use on 11th. May 1907 as a joint operation with the L & Y. The NER had its own steamship which plied to various ports, while Messrs. Thomas Wilson & Co. sailed to Hamburg, Antwerp, Ghent and Dunkirk. Three times weekly the 'Duke of Clarence' crossed to and from Zeebrugge, a port largely built up by the L & Y, and boat trains were run on both side of the North sea in connection with this facility. Here, there were through coaches from Glasgow, Newcastle, York and Selby, also Liverpool Exchange, Manchester, Wakefield and Goole. The various timetables do not always make the service clear, though interesting when deciphered, as in September 1926 when there was a 5.23 p.m. arrival at the waterside with through carriages from King's Cross and Barry and a 10.42 a.m. out to Sheffield Vic. which conveyed a through coach to Barry. For the Tuesday only, 21st. September there was an entry for a departure from the Quay at 7.50 a.m., arriving Paragon station at 8.02 a.m., to connect with the 9.00 a.m. to Liverpool Lime St. (Brough at 9.15 a.m. to take up only). This was probably part of the arrangements for a special cruise. Why Barry was singled out for regular through coaches is rather strange.

Alexandra Dock was ready for use on 7th. August 1885. The railway station was, as described earlier, in the north west corner by the signal box. It was mainly noted for the emigrant traffic, with which ships would arrive on Fridays or Saturdays, the emigrants spending two or three nights in Hull, sometimes camping out in Pearson park. Special trains would leave Cannon Street for Liverpool on Monday mornings, as that station was more convenient for transfer. On 13th. Octover 1907 the 'Edouard Regal' arrived with 404 from Russia; then 346 came on 28th. October and further 495 on 10th. November. Traffic was intermittent up to 1914 and was transported in four wheelers which would have to be made available.

The H & BR advertised heavily their bi-weekly excursions to Brussels via Cannon Street, in 1907 Yorkshire to Hamburg from Leeds via Alexandra Dock was 33/- available on Weds. and Sats., among many others quoted. The same from Dublin was 50/-.

Riverside Quay was given a battering by the enemy during the 1939-45 war, and was completely destroyed. However, to enable soldiers returning home from the continent via Cuxhaven, five Mulberry pontoons were moored alongside the site to enable unloading to take place.

The railway in wartime

Wartime presented many new and unheard of problems for the railways, as well as the chief one of survival. There was no lighting in marshalling yards, while engines had tarpaulins draped from cab to tender to keep down firebox glare and the heat in at night, rather unpleasant in summer. Stations were dimly lit and not named, so that drivers had carefully to draw up so as to bring the train in line with the platform ends. After November trains were to run at 25 mph in daylight and 15 mph at night, once a warning of an air raid had been received. Freight was timed at 15 mph day and night. After 1941 trains could run normally at night, reducing to 30 mph in raids. Where some lighting was allowed in yards, this was dimmed even further during a 'purple' alert, and extinguished during a 'red', when bombers were close by. Enemy flares often provided unwittingly welcome illumination.

Hull merits a book of its own on air raids received; it had over one hundred by February 1944 during 850 alerts. The worst night was 7th. May 1941 when much of the city centre was ablaze and some fine shops disappeared for ever. The station was peppered with incendiary bombs and fires were started in the roof; these were fought at first from the platforms using hose jets. Messrs. Dickinson, Coultas, Arridge and Smith were on duty and climbed on to a waiting room roof, them after difficulties broke a window of the main roof with a ladder and climbed out, where they spent a merry hour or two rolling about in the gutters and ridging smothering the wretched devices. Apart from the north east corner which contained a small railway museum, they can be considered as the men who saved the station that night.

The station signal box had a landmine dropped next to it, which cracked the walls, brought down the ceiling and shattered the windows. Lineman Greenlees was on hand to repair the damaged circuitry and switchgear, while ¼ in. steel shutters which were available for such an emergency were fixed at the windows. The cabin was out of action for only 1½ hours that night. Down the line at West Parade signalman Shipley found himself in his wooden cabin next to an inferno when the timber yard close by went up, also that his only free route was that to and from Selby.

At Victoria dock at the time when all its timber stock was destroyed were Messrs. Filby, Tawlkes and McBain. They did what they could but soon gave up against the odds and eventually had to crawl down a slipway beneath a ship to escape. Constable Dobson of the railway police had a go, with two others, at saving Riverside Quay when it was destroyed. His mates were buried at one time, so he called up a rescue team and helped them to dig them out, later rescuing a fireman who had been blown by a bomb into one of the fires. He received the BEM for his deeds. Constable Wright manhandled burning wagons beneath a water crane on the docks, to extinguish them.

There was a chaotic mess at Kingston Street goods warehouse after one raid, with a mixture of rail and road vehicles under a mass of collapsed roofing. Much was salvaged, either by bringing up locomotives or sheer manhandling. The Yardmaster was called out to supervise but never arrived–he had fallen into a bomb crater!

During the summer of 1941 many Hull folk crowded Paragon station to overfill the evening trains out to the country districts in order to sleep out in the fields, such was the fear of the bombing raids. This put great strain on the staff who had to issue many tickets and provide extra trains in some cases.

Belatedly the Government ordered the dispersal of timber from Hull to protect remaining stocks from air-raids. Thus stocks were to be found at places like Sandholme and Gilberdyke.

It is a tribute to all concerned that staff undertook tasks which were beyond the call of duty in many cases, in an effort to keep things moving, and there was no pilfering, even though opportunities galore cropped up.

There were armoured trains available in the Hull area, more to combat any likelihood of invasion by the enemy than to offer any form of attack. 'Armoured Train H' was stationed at Market Weighton for the second half of 1940, one of twelve trains hastily assembled to counter the threat of invasion, fitted with an old six pounder at each end of the train, between which were LMS wagons protected by 4 in. of concrete. Two of them carried stores and repair materials for the railway track, while in the centre the motive power was an old, amour plated great Eastern engine. There were also machine guns on board, manned by men of the Royal Tank Regiment, while the Royal Engineers operated the locomotive. Once a week the train ran along the coast lines out to Hornsea, Withernsea and Scarborough. The Sixth Super Heavy Battery RA (good Boys' Own stuff, this) came to Willerby station in July 1940, bringing two rail mounted 12" howitzers, one located there, the other up at Little Weighton with a further firing position at Kirkella cutting. In the event of invasion, 750 lb shells were available for firing at and neutralising Hull docks and Anlaby aerodrome. Later, the equipment was moved to Goxhill and Ulceby on the south bank where one assumes it could be just as effective.

Accidents

The railways round Hull have been remarkably free from serious accidents over the years, with the exception perhaps of that at Lockington recently when a dmu ran into a vehicle on one of the newly installed unmanned automatic crossings, causing some loss of life. There was

D49 No. 62765 "The Goathland" heads a line of combined fellows at Springhead. On the right is a line of B16s. *C. T. Goode*

also a similar occurrence involving a trans-pennine unit late at night at Welton, again where a vehicle was involved. However, there are two 'classic' accidents which will stand repeating:

On Wednesday, 23rd. December 1903 the 4.50 p.m. for Hull left Cudworth headed by 2-4-0 No. 34, made up of five four wheelers and fish van. The train was running between Willerby and Locomotive Jc. when it ran into the rear portion of a Down special coal train from Denaby to Alexandra Dock which had come adrift due to a broken coupling link on the 17th. wagon of the 28 forming the train. The engine was severely damaged, turning over and blocking the other line. The driver was seriously injured and, of the 15 passengers, three were also injured. The guard of the coal train, George Paddison, was able to leap from his van before the impact took place, which smashed it and the last three wagons to pieces. Thos. Littlewood, fireman of the passenger train, gave the following statement at the enquiry: 'I remember our arriving at Willerby, and I think that it was about 6.55 p.m. My train was brought to a stand at the Willerby starting signal and we remained standing there for about eight minutes. When the starting signal was lowered we released our brakes. I remember approaching the distant signal for Locomotive Jc. When I first sighted those distant signals they were both at danger. We were about 50 or 60 yards away from them when I first sighted them Immediately I whistled the main line distant was lowered for us, consequently we did not check the speed of our train in any way. The first I knew of there being anything on the line in front of me was seeing the lights of a brake van. When I first saw them I at once shouted to my mate (driver Pearce) 'Whoa'. My mate at once shut off steam and applied the brake, and I also applied the hand brake. I think we reduced our speed a little before the collision occurred, but we were going pretty fast when it did actually occur. My driver was still on the engine after I had gone to the signalman in front to warn him; my mate was so injured that he was helpless'.

A rather more serious accident happened on 14th. February 1927, in which 12 passengers died and 24 were seriously injured. A train for Scarborough had just departed from Hull and was passing Park Street signal box just outside. As a Withernsea arrival was approaching, the signalmen were too quick at replacing the signal to danger behind the first train, which allowed them to change a cross over in front of it which put it on the arrival side instead of departure; it was now on the same line as the approaching Withernsea train. The driver, Sam Atkinson realised fairly quickly that he was on the wrong line of the seven in the layout at this point, shut off steam and braked, but was unable to avoid a collision. Both engines, Class D22 No. 96 and Class D17 No.1628 were badly damaged and written off.

It is pleasant to finish on a cheerful note. Mr Bourne was Ticket Collector at Paragon station during the time that Mr Baines was station master. That elegant, bowler hatted gentleman always saw the principal train in and out of the platforms, and run a friendly but strict regime. Mr. Bourne sends a few anecdotes, one of which tells of the time when he was on mornings at Platform 8, where the train to Doncaster, a slow one, was waiting to leave. Suddely, just as the whistles were blowing, a couple of Signal & Telegraph men, bound for Goole rolled up with their tools. Quickly they were told to pile into the last compartment; the signal was given and the train set off, leaving the last coach behind, which had just been 'stopped' by the carriage examiner for a dud wheel bearing and detached without notifying the platform staff. No further comment on reactions is needed.

The present arrangements for running Hull's trains are generally very satisfactory, as a visit to Paragon station or a trip on one of the services will soon prove. Trains are normally well used and such benefits as air conditioning and on-board telephones were unknown a year or two ago. The new 158 units reach Leeds in just one hour and Manchester in two, and are comfortable, though tight on knee room in places. The regular departure times are to be commended, though what can ruin time keeping os the fact that Hull depends on the prompt arrival of an incoming service to turn it round into a promt departure. No spare trains sets are kept at this end-the branch line mentality is slow to die.

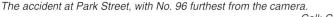

The accident at Park Street, with No. 96 furthest from the camera.
Coll: C.T. Goode

Round and about there is little left of the old railway scene, except perhaps the station buildings at Beverley, Hedon, Hessle, Little Weighton and Ferriby, plus the interesting one at Stepney. The H & B bridges linger on, and if one waits long enough beneath one and uses a little imagination, then along will come the shade of an old Stirling domeless 0-6-0, trundling its load of coal wagons.

Q679X (HD)

BRITISH RAILWAYS

EXCURSIONS

TO

HULL

EVERY WEEKDAY

JULY 2nd to SEPTEMBER 8th

(INCLUSIVE)

OUTWARD					THIRD RETURN	RETURN
		a.m.	a.m.	p.m.	s. d.	
Scarborough ...	dep.	—	11 30	1 3	6 6	
Seamer	,,	—	11 37	1 9	6 3	PASSENGERS MAY
Filey	,,	—	11 54	1 24	5 9	
Hunmanby ...	,,	—	12 0	1 30	5 3	RETURN BY ANY
			p.m.			
Speeton	,,	—	—	1 38	5 0	ORDINARY
Bempton	,,	—	12 13	1 44	4 9	
Flamborough ...	,,	—	12 16	1 47	4 6	TRAIN
Bridlington ...	,,	10 52	12 24	1 55	4 0	
Carnaby	,,	—	—	2 0	3 9	ON DAY OF
Burton Agnes	,,	—	12 33	—	3 6	
Lowthorpe ...	,,	—	12 37	2 8	3 6	ISSUE
Nafferton ...	,,	—	12 42	2 13	3 0	
Driffield	,,	11 9	12 49	2 20	2 9	
Hutton Cranswick	,,	—	12 55	2 26	2 6	
Lockington ...	,,	—	1 1	2 32	2 0	
Arram	,,	—	1 6	2 37	1 9	
Hull	arr	11 39	1 30	3 0	—	

TICKETS CAN BE OBTAINED IN ADVANCE

at the stations

Further information will be supplied on application to the stations, or to the District Commercial Superintendent, 109 George Street, Hull, Tel 31739 (Ext. 17), or York, Tel. 53022 (Ext. 397).

FESTIVAL OF BRITAIN ATTRACTIONS IN LONDON

May—September, 1951

Numerous excursions will be run from the provincial towns to London in connection with the above, and full details thereof will be announced from time to time as the event approaches.

Inclusive arrangements, embracing rail transport and meals, booking of "advance" Admission Tickets to the SOUTH BANK EXHIBITION, and other services, will be undertaken on behalf of organised parties offering a minimum of eight adult passengers.

Secretaries of clubs, works outings and other organisations are invited to make known their travel etc. requirements in good time by communicating with the District Passenger Superintendents at Newcastle or Leeds, the District Commercial Superintendents at Hull, Middlesbrough or York, or the local Station Master.

CONDITIONS OF ISSUE

These tickets are issued subject to the conditions of issue of ordinary passenger tickets where applicable, and also to the special conditions as set out in the Bye-Laws, Regulations and Conditions in the Published Notices of the Railway Executive

LUGGAGE ALLOWANCES are as set out in these general notices

Published by the Railway Executive N.E Region) 7/51 Printed in Gt. Britain Youngman Ltd., Leeds. 2500

DEPARTURE OF TRAINS

FROM

FERRIBY

THE TELEPHONE NUMBER OF THIS STATION IS HULL 631330

5 SEPTEMBER 1966 TO 5 MARCH 1967

DOWN PLATFORM

WEEKDAYS

HOUR	DOWN PLATFORM
07 22	**Hessle 07 27, Hull 07 35**
07 29	**Hessle 07 34, Hull 07 42**
07 58	*Saturdays excepted* **Hessle 08 03, Hull 08 11,** Bridlington, Filey, Scarborough
08 26	**Hessle 08 31, Hull 08 41**
08 36	**Hessle 08 41, Hull 08 51**
09 13	**Hessle 09 18, Hull 09 26**
10 00	**Hessle 10 05, Hull 10 16,** Bridlington, Filey, Scarborough
11 27	*Saturdays excepted* **Hessle 11 32, Hull 11 40**
12 03	*Saturdays only* **Hessle 12 08, Hull 12 16,** Bridlington, Filey, Scarborough
12 05	*Saturdays excepted* **Hessle 12 10, Hull 12 18,** Bridlington,
12 50	*Saturdays only* **Hessle 12 55, Hull 13 04,** Bridlington, Filey, Scarborough
13 42	*Saturdays excepted* **Hessle 13 47, Hull 13 58**
13 45	*Saturdays only* **Hessle 13 50, Hull 13 59**
14 09	*Fridays and Saturdays excepted* **Hessle 14 14, Hull 14 22**
14 17	*Fridays only* **Hessle 14 22, Hull 14 30**
14 26	*Saturdays only* **Hessle 14 31, Hull 14 40**
16 16	**Hessle 16 21, Hull 16 29,** Bridlington
16 28	*Saturdays only* **Hessle 16 33, Hull 16 43**
16 53	*Saturdays excepted* **Hessle 16 58, Hull 17 06,** Bridlington, Filey, Scarborough
16 58	**Hessle 17 03, Hull 17 13,** (except Saturdays) Bridlington
17 21	*Saturdays excepted* **Hessle 17 26, Hull 17 34,** Bridlington, Filey, Scarborough
17 38	*Saturdays excepted* **Hessle 17 43, Hull 17 51**
18 09	**Hessle 18 14, Hull 18 25**
18 17	**Hessle 18 22, Hull 18 30,** Bridlington
19 28	**Hessle 19 33, Hull 19 41,** Bridlington
21 01	**Hessle 21 06, Hull 21 15,** Bridlington
22 40	**Hessle 22 45, Hull 22 53**

UP PLATFORM

WEEKDAYS

HOUR	UP PLATFORM
06 29	**Rotherham 08 08, and intermediate stations** (except Broomfleet) **Sheffield (Mid.) 08 20,** Manchester Piccadilly
07 04	**Leeds City 08 35 and intermediate stations** (except Broomfleet) Manchester Exchange, Liverpool Lime Street
07 11	**Goole 07 40 and intermediate stations**
07 29	**Doncaster 08 33 and intermediate stations** (except Barnby Dun), London King's Cross
08 10	**Leeds City 09 32 and intermediate stations, Dewsbury Wellington Road 10 01, Huddersfield 10 14, Stalybridge 10 42, Manchester Exchange 10 58**
08 19	*Saturdays excepted* **Goole 08 48 and intermediate stations**
08 39	**Brough 08 46, Selby 09 06,** Doncaster, Peterborough, London King's Cross
09 59	*Saturdays only* **Goole 10 26 and intermediate stations**
11 14	*Saturdays only* **Rotherham 12 58 and intermediate stations** (except Stainforth and Barnby Dun), **Sheffield Midland 13 16,** change Doncaster for London King's Cross
12 44	*Fridays only* **Brough 12 49**
12 44	*Saturdays only* **Selby 13 33 and intermediate stations,** Leeds City, Manchester Exchange, Liverpool Lime Street
12 46	*Fridays and Saturdays excepted* **Brough 12 53,**
13 34	*Saturdays excepted* **Brough 13 41,** Selby, Leeds City, Manchester Exchange, Liverpool Lime Street, **Goole 13 56 and intermediate stations to Wakefield Westgate 14 59**
13 48	*Saturdays only* **Doncaster 14 52 and intermediate stations** (except Barnby Dun) Sheffield Midland
14 22	*Saturdays excepted* **Goole 14 49 and intermediate stations,** Doncaster, Peterborough, London King's Cross, Sheffield
14 46	*Saturdays only* **Leeds City 16 07 and intermediate stations** (except Broomfleet)
14 46	*Saturdays excepted* **Selby 15 28 and intermediate stations** (except Broomfleet), Leeds City
16 29	*Saturdays only* **Doncaster 17 36 and intermediate stations,** Sheffield Midland (change at Brough for Selby, Leeds, Manchester, Liverpool)
16 34	*Saturdays excepted* **Brough 16 40**
17 04	*Saturdays excepted* **Goole 17 33 and intermediate stations,** Doncaster, Peterborough, London King's Cross (Change at Brough for Selby, Leeds, Manchester, Liverpool
17 34	**Brough 17 41, Broomfleet 17 49, Staddlethorpe 17 54, Selby 18 09**
18 09	**Brough 18 14, Broomfleet 18 21, Staddlethorpe 18 26, Eastrington 18 31, Howden 18 37, Selby 18 49, South Milford 19 03, Micklefield 19 10, Garforth 19 15, Cross Gates 19 21, Leeds City 19 28, Dewsbury 20 00, Huddersfield 20 14, Stalybridge 20 41, Manchester Exchange 20 56, Earlestown 21 19, St. Helens Junction 21 23, Liverpool Lime St. 21 41**
18 34	**Goole 19 01 and intermediate stations, Knottingley 19 26, Pontefract Monkhill 19 30, Wakefield Kirkgate 19 45**
19 18	**Doncaster 20 26 and intermediate stations** (except Barnby Dun), **Sheffield Midland 21 21**
21 45	**Brough 21 52, Broomfleet 21 58, Staddlethorpe 22 03, Selby 22 18, Cross Gates 22 45, Leeds City 22 52**
23 01	*Saturdays only* **Goole 23 28 and intermediate stations**

Through carriages to stations shown in **bold type**

Time of arrival is shown after the station name

The train services shown here are subject to alteration or cancellation at short notice, and do not necessarily apply at Bank and Public Holiday Periods

No. 84

BRITISH RAILWAYS

No. 208

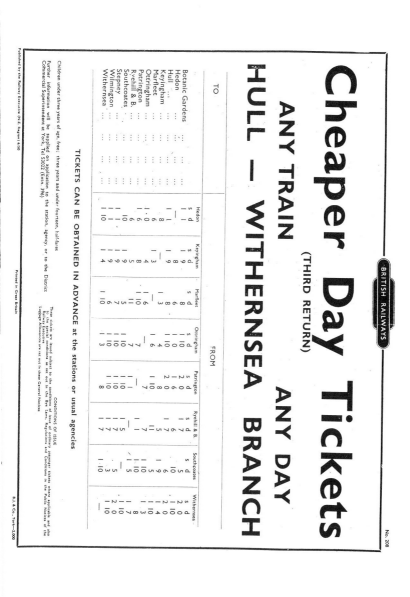

Cheaper Day Tickets

(THIRD RETURN)

ANY TRAIN ANY DAY

HULL — WITHERNSEA BRANCH

TO	FROM: Hedon	Keyingham	Marfleet	Ottringham	Patrington	Ryehill & B.	Southcoates	Withernsea
	s d	s d	s d	s d	s d	s d	s d	s d
Botanic Gardens	1 1	1 9	8	1 10	2 0	1 7	5	2 0
Hedon	—	8	6	1 0	1 6	6	10	1 10
Hull	1 1	1 9	8	1 10	2 0	1 7	6	2 0
Keyingham	8	—	1 3	4	8	5	1 9	1 4
Marfleet	6	1 3	—	1 6	1 10	11	5	1 10
Ottringham	1 0	4	1 6	—	7	7	1 10	1 3
Patrington	1 6	8	1 10	7	—	1 1	1 10	8
Ryehill & B.	6	5	11	7	1 1	—	1 5	1 7
Southcoates	10	1 9	5	1 10	1 10	1 5	—	1 10
Stepney	1 1	1 9	7	1 10	1 10	1 7	5	2 0
Wilmington	1 1	1 9	6	1 10	1 10	1 7	3	1 10
Withernsea	1 10	1 4	1 10	1 3	8	1 7	1 10	—

TICKETS CAN BE OBTAINED IN ADVANCE at the stations or usual agencies

Children under three years of age, free; three years and under fourteen, half-fares

Further information will be supplied on application to the station, agency, or to the District Commercial Superintendent at York, Tel 53022 (Extn. 396)

CONDITIONS OF ISSUE

These tickets are issued subject to the conditions of issue of ordinary passenger tickets where applicable and also to the special conditions as set out in the Bye Laws, Regulations and Conditions in the Public Notices of the Railway Executive

Luggage Allowances are set out in these General Notices

Published by the Railway Executive (N.E. Region) 6/50

Printed in Great Britain

B.J. & Co., York—2,000

NOTES